Offshore Windpower

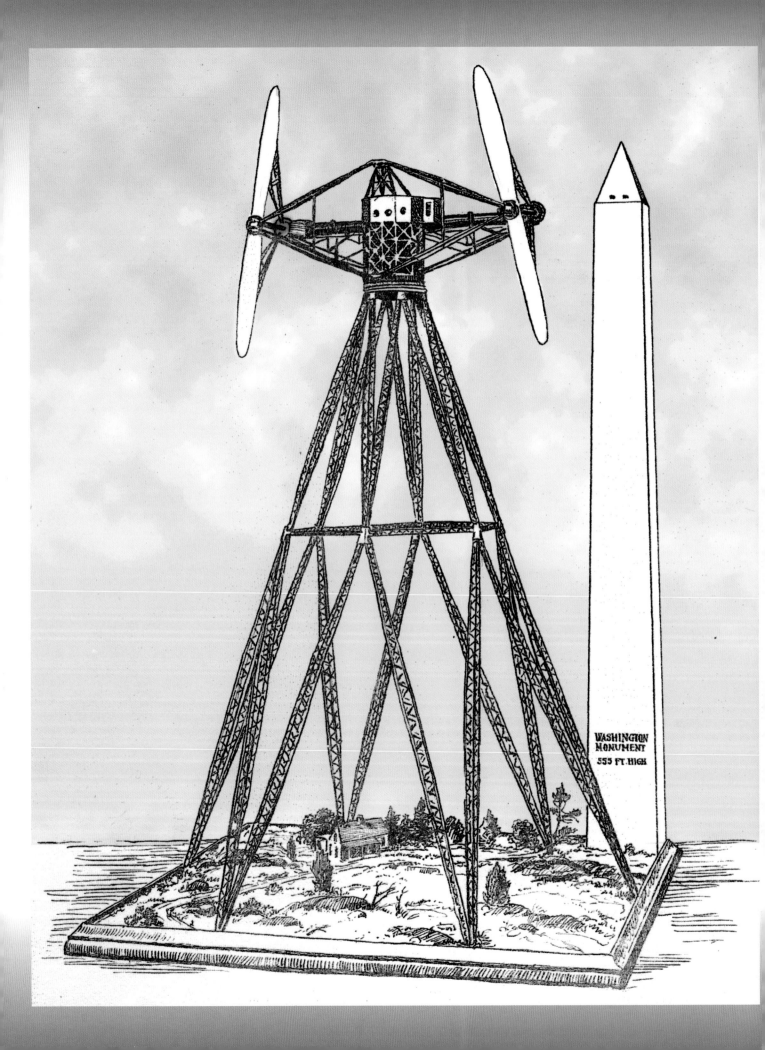

WASHINGTON
MONUMENT
555 FT. HIGH

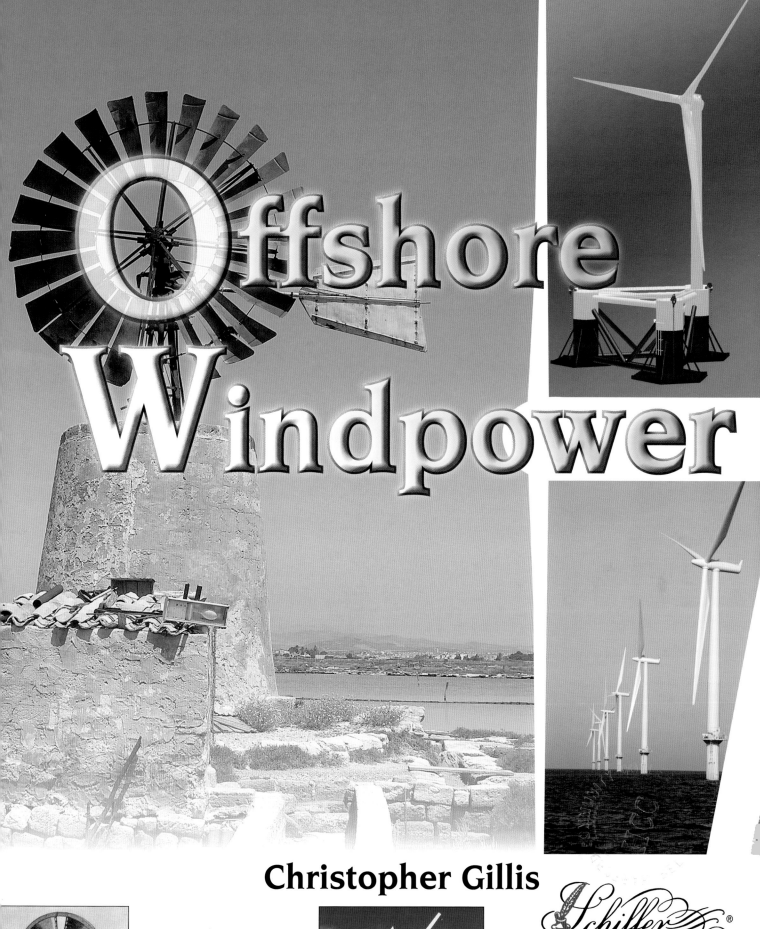

Offshore Windpower

Christopher Gillis

Schiffer Publishing Ltd

4880 Lower Valley Road, Atglen, Pennsylvania 19310

Schiffer Books are available at special discounts for bulk purchases for sales promotions or premiums. Special editions, including personalized covers, corporate imprints, and excerpts can be created in large quantities for special needs. For more information contact the publisher:

Published by Schiffer Publishing Ltd.
4880 Lower Valley Road
Atglen, PA 19310
Phone: (610) 593-1777; Fax: (610) 593-2002
E-mail: Info@schifferbooks.com

For the largest selection of fine reference books on this and related subjects, please visit our website at:
www.schifferbooks.com
We are always looking for people to write books on new and related subjects. If you have an idea for a book please contact us at the above address.

This book may be purchased from the publisher.
Include $5.00 for shipping.
Please try your bookstore first.
You may write for a free catalog.

In Europe, Schiffer books are distributed by
Bushwood Books
6 Marksbury Ave.
Kew Gardens
Surrey TW9 4JF England
Phone: 44 (0) 20 8392 8585; Fax: 44 (0) 20 8392 9876
E-mail: info@bushwoodbooks.co.uk
Website: www.bushwoodbooks.co.uk

Contents

Acknowledgments

The purpose of this book is to provide a basic overview of how offshore wind energy and its technology have evolved in application — not just in North America, but also globally. It's neither a definitive historical account nor a technical manual. The goal is simply to provide a pathway for readers to learn the basics about this increasingly important energy source and generate sufficient interest to seek out additional works by noted authors in the field and Internet-based sources for more in-depth knowledge and understanding.

It must also be pointed out that this book would not have been possible without the kind assistance and support of numerous government and industry experts, historians, and friends.

In the area of offshore wind energy history and early pioneers, I received support from Dr. T. Lindsay Baker, author and editor of the *Windmillers' Gazette*; Frans Brouwers, editor of *Levende Molens*; windmill historians George Speis of Greece, and Michael Haverson and Fred Atkins, both of the United Kingdom; and Fr. Elias Yelovich, research librarian at Mount St. Mary's University in Emmitsburg, Maryland. I would like to thank Dietmar Jost of Düsseldorf, Germany, for his patient translations of World War II-era documents from German to English, and for the constant encouragement of my friends Johan Copermans and Peter Neyens in Belgium.

Marcia Heronemus-Pate, chief executive officer of OWES, LLC, in Tulsa, Oklahoma, generously shared numerous recollections, documents, articles, and photographs of her late father, William E. Heronemus, the former Navy captain and University of Massachusetts at Amherst professor who, in the early 1970s, opened the world's eyes to the potential for clean energy benefits from large-scale offshore wind turbines. The "Wind King," as he became known, carried on this message until his death in 2002.

During my research, I was fortunate to connect with Staffan Engström, managing director of Lidingö, Sweden-based Ägir konsult AB, who kindly shared his experiences in helping to build the world's first modern offshore wind turbine near the Swedish town of Nogersund in 1990 and agreed to write the Foreword for this book. Other industry pioneers to assist me were Dr. Peter Musgrove, who was instrumental in encouraging the United Kingdom to embrace offshore wind energy in the 1990s, and Peter Christiansen, project manager, SEAS-NVE Holding A/S, who participated in the construction of the world's first offshore wind farm at Vindeby, Denmark, in 1991.

With Europe being the leader in offshore wind energy development, I relied on the Global Wind Energy Council and European Wind Energy Association, both based in Brussels, Belgium, and the Danish Wind Industry Association in Frederiksberg, Denmark, for the latest facts, figures, industry and academic contacts, and photos. Frank Coenen, chief executive officer for Belwind in Zeebrugge, Belgium, took me step-by-step through the process of building an offshore wind farm. In North America, I received invaluable information and illustrations from the U.S. government's National Renewable Energy Laboratory and wind farm developers such as Cape Wind, Deepwater, and WEST. Prof. Hikaru Matsumiya, an expert on the Japanese wind energy industry, and He Dexin, president of the Chinese Wind Energy Association, shared with me information about offshore wind developments in their respective countries.

While researching the history of small wind machines for offshore applications, I relied on the expertise of Craig Toepfer, author of the recently published *Hybrid Electric Home* (Schiffer Publishing Ltd., 2010). In-depth interviews with Andy Kruse of Southwest Windpower in Flagstaff, Arizona, and Pete Anderson of Eclectic Energy Ltd., Ollerton, United Kingdom, provided details into how today's small offshore wind turbines provide power to sailboats and yachts, as well as industrial applications.

My ability to write knowledgably about the offshore transportation of wind turbine components comes from my fifteen years with *American Shipper* magazine. Through this venue, I encountered numerous experts involved in turbine manufacturing, marine terminal management, and vessel transportation. Their names are found throughout *Chapter 5* of this book.

I want to especially acknowledge my friends Keith Higginbotham in Long Beach, California, and Mike Bowersox in Frederick, Maryland, for their generous help during the evenings and weekends with evaluating, scanning, and preparing the very best illustrations for this book. I could not have done it without them.

Most importantly, I would like to thank my family and friends who quietly endured the numerous hours that I spent grinding away at this book. My wife, Theresa, and children, Christopher and Elizabeth, were most encouraging and loving through the entire process.

Foreword

Offshore windpower represents the ultimate dream of tapping nature's resources for renewable energy without polluting and endangering wildlife, and without conflict with other human interests. But as with all dreams, reality demonstrates that there are always conflicts when trying to realize large infrastructure projects. You are always in someone's backyard, no matter how remote the project may seem. Everywhere someone has an interest to guard, or at least he or she believes that to be the case. And if this isn't enough, there is often a conflict between the value of the electricity that can be tapped versus the investments and maintenance required to generate it.

Yet offshore windpower persists today, thanks to the many men and women who take on these challenges; find solutions to the technical, legal, and economical problems; and, at best, make friends with those who opposed the idea in the beginning. To achieve these goals, the people involved must be competent in their areas, and still this is not enough. In order to be successful in a pioneering field such as offshore wind energy, one must be engaged in a personal way to overcome numerous obstacles. A revolutionary spirit is needed.

Compared to onshore, offshore wind is generally stronger and more consistent. The problem with this form of renewable energy currently resides in the excess costs to build sub-sea foundations, lay power cables, erect the wind turbines and above all ensure adequate maintenance availability to ensure continuous production. This means that, at least for the foreseeable future, offshore wind power will be costlier than those wind turbines operating onshore. Yet it is still extremely worthwhile in regions where onshore wind resources are either meager or depleted, which is the case for many areas across Europe, North America, and other developed regions in the world.

Last year, wind energy covered 1.6 percent of the world's electricity consumption. By 2020, the Danish consulting firm, BTM Consult, estimates that it will reach eight percent, which means a contribution in the same order of magnitude in 2008 as hydro (sixteen percent), according to BP's Statistical Review of World Energy 2009) and nuclear (fourteen percent). Obviously offshore wind will have an important role in realizing these very large contributions to the world's energy supply.

When writing this historic account on offshore wind energy, Christopher Gillis puts words on the efforts needed for this evolution in electric power generation. He also demonstrates that spirit exhibited by those pioneers in the field by contributing to the general public's understanding of offshore wind technology, which will surely prove important to the future of mankind.

—Staffan Engström
Managing Director
Ägir konsult AB
Lidingö, Sweden
June 2010

Chapter One

Ocean Breezes

The air is constantly moving in the form of wind. Sometimes you barely feel its motion against your skin, while in some instances it may be powerful enough to knock you down. The wind's free availability and abundance has inspired humans for more than 1,000 years to develop ways to exploit the energy for use. Perhaps nowhere on the planet are we more reminded of this awesome force then along a large lake or ocean shore or out on a boat. Here, the wind sweeps across the water's surface unobstructed. The strength of the wind varies according to atmospheric temperatures. Wind is essentially generated when the sun heats the earth's surface, forming large areas of high pressure that move to areas of lower pressure, or cooler air masses, seeking atmospheric equilibrium.

While no one will ever know for sure who was first to harness the wind, it was likely the ancient mariners who developed sails to propel their vessels forward on the sea. The first landside application of wind in the form of windmills is undefined. However, the earliest references to windmills point to the remote, rugged border of modern day Pakistan and Afghanistan. Here, perhaps twelve centuries ago, the inhabitants erected horizontal windmills, meaning that a set of light-weight sails mostly made from reeds were spaced within a cylinder, which in turn drove a vertical shaft leading to a set of millstones. Persia's early horizontal windmills are mentioned in a text from 950 AD referring to the tales of the Banu Musa brothers of Baghdad between 850 and 870 AD. About 1300, Mohammed Al Dimasshqi offered a detailed description of a horizontal windmill in his book *Nukhbat-al-Dahr* (translated *Stories of the Centuries*). A drawing shows the windmill with millstones on the top floor and a horizontal wind wheel. The building surrounding the mill had several long vertical slots in the walls to channel wind to the wind wheel.[1]

It's equally unclear when the Europeans first acquired windmill technology and if it had any connection to the return of the crusaders from the Middle East at around 1100 AD, as originally believed by some early historians. Documentation studied in more recent years has found references to windmills in Europe at the time of the crusades and fifty to one hundred years earlier. The early European windmill is also distinctly different from its Middle Eastern counterpart. There are three primary types of windmill structures that emerged in the Middle Ages:

Post

Perhaps the earliest known style of windmill on the continent, the squared wooden housing, which contains the gearing, millstones, and other equipment, is erected upon a heavy wood post. This allows the housing to be turned so that the sails can catch the wind.

Tower

These cylindrical or cone-shaped structures were composed of either wood or stone. These windmills could be built taller and stronger than post windmills. While the towers were stationary, the caps through which the sails protruded could be rotated into the wind.

Smock

By the 1600s, wood-framed towers, which from a distance resembled a man's work smock, were erected in northern Europe. Smock windmills were often constructed with octagonal sides that sloped at the bottom. They were faced with boards and, some cases, with thatch.

By the 1600s and 1700s, windmills were used for a variety of industrial applications beyond just grinding grains into flour, including crushing oil seeds and oak bark for leather tanning, sawing wood, shaping brass, making fertilizer, producing textiles, and pumping water.

Proximity of Europe's early windmills to the coast was determined by geography. Windmills were located on the shores of what are modern-day Greece, Spain, Portugal, Italy, France and the United Kingdom. A necessary condition for building windmills close to the sea is stable ground. The Mediterranean and British Isles offer hard, rocky coastlines suitable for large heavy buildings like windmills. The Low Countries of Belgium and the Netherlands, on the other hand, have sandy, less stable coastlines. A post windmill might have been suitable within these coastal conditions as long as the miller was prepared to occasionally move the structure with the shifting dune on which it was standing.[2] In this region, normally windmills were constructed several kilometers away from the coastline on dykes or "terpen," which were small manmade earthen mounds.[3]

MILL AT ST.-SERVAN.

An engraving of the old windmill at Saint-Servan, a town in western France's Brittany region, which is located about two miles from the ferry port of St Malo. Published in the book *Picturesque Europe* in 1874.

Friedhof der Heimatlosen a. Nordseeinsel Amrum

3313

This windmill is on the German North Sea Coastal island of Amrum. Postcard c. 1950.

Coxyde s/Mer   Le Moulin De Blekker dans les dunes.

This windmill, in the dunes along the Belgian coast at Coxyde, was
severely damaged by German artillery in 1940. Postcard (c. 1905) depicts
windmill before the war.

Arribana de milho e moinho de vento. — S. Miguel-Açores.
Maize-farm and Wind-mill. — S. Michael-Azores.

Windmill for grinding corn on the island of São Miguel in the Azores. Postcard c. 1905.

Windmills at the salt works in Aden, a seaport city in Yemen, located at the eastern approach to the Red Sea. Postcard c. 1920.

Coastal windmills located at Trapani, Sicily, once used for lifting saltwater into shallow reservoirs for salt production.
Courtesy of Jan Althof, Zwijndrecht, the Netherlands.

15

The Greek windmill, with its stone cylindrical shaped tower, became a feature along the country's highly populated coastal mainland and islands. The oldest known document on record referring to a windmill in Greece's Salonica region comes from 1302. Greek windmills were generally controlled by wealthy owners, who rented them to professional millers for the manufacture of flour. In a few cases, they were owned by the Orthodox Church.[4] Windmills in Greece were also employed for other purposes, such as grinding materials for the tanning industry on the island of Chios.[5] The northerly winds from the Greek seas are local in nature. In some island locations the winds were so consistent that the mill builders had no need to construct mechanisms to turn the sails into the wind. It's interesting to note that while Greek windmills, as well as others scattered throughout the Mediterranean,

today are known for their wispy cloth or jib sails, that's not the way many of them operated prior to the mid-1800s. These windmills formerly had the heavier wood lattice sails like those commonly found in northern Europe. However, lattice sails were expensive to maintain, and as heavy timber became scarce throughout the Mediterranean, windmill operators replaced these sails with slender spars consisting of eight to ten jib sails.[6] The remnants of these windmills, mostly in the form of their squat stone towers, may be found throughout the Greek islands. According to the Greek Molinological Society, only about ten windmills are in actual operational condition in the country today.[7] In places such as Portugal, Spain, France, the Azores, and even Bulgaria, there are still examples of windmills constructed with round stone bases topped with a rotatable wooden housing containing the milling equipment and jib sails.[8]

Numerous small stone tower windmills once dotted the Greek islands. A windmill overlooks the waters off Mykonos (Postcard c. 1940), while a row of windmills stand next to a lighthouse on the island of Rhodes (Postcard c. 1910).

Rodi - Esterno Torre degli Angeli

17

5. Вѣтърна мелница край Созополъ.   • Sozopol.

A "composite" windmill, with its narrow stone base supporting a rotating wooden mill house along the coast of Sozopol, Bulgaria. Postcard c. 1905.

By the late 1600s and early 1700s, Europeans began to transfer their windmill technology to the Americas. Dutch settlers, in what is today Lower Manhattan, New York, built a windmill in 1621 to take advantage of the winds off the harbor. While examples of these windmills were found throughout North America and the Caribbean, New England and the Mid-Atlantic states became the home for numerous small near-shore windmills. Some windmills were even constructed close to the shores of the Great Lakes.

This old smock-style windmill was located at Chatham on Cape Cod, Massachusetts. Postcard c. 1910.

Windmill overlooking the bluff at Montauk Point, Long Island, New York. Postcard c. 1910.

This old windmill was located along the water at Leesburg, New Jersey, in the early 1900s. Postcard c. 1910.

This windmill, photographed by Dr. L. V. Morgan, was located at Point Breeze at the southern entrance of Milford Haven along the Virginia shore. In its day, this wooden structure must have been a welcome landmark for those seeking safe shelter during a storm. Its remains were washed away in a 1933 flood. The place where the foundation stood is now far out in the Milford Haven.
Courtesy of the Mathews County Historical Society, Mathews, Virginia.

An American style, all steel-framed windmill for pumping water took advantage of the lake breezes while operating on Dollar Island within the Les Cheneaux Islands, Michigan in the early 1900s. Postcard c. 1910.

One of the more interesting examples of early American windmills taking advantage of sea breezes was the style of those constructed on the island of Martha's Vineyard to pump saltwater into wooden vats on shore for salt production. In 1776, the island's inhabitants risked starvation, and it was impossible to obtain the salt used for food preservation from the mainland due to the British blockade. Salt was also crucial to leather tanning and medicinal ingredients. Salt production techniques at the time included boiling sea water, but the yield was not sufficient and timely enough to meet the island population's needs.

Thus Captain John Sears of Dennis, Massachusetts, devised a system of large wooden vats to hold seawater and used sunlight to evaporate the moisture, leaving behind a coating of salt that could be scraped away. This method was soon combined with a water-pumping windmill attributed to Major Nathaniel Freeman of Harwich, Massachusetts, and the concept spread throughout Cape Cod and the other neighboring islands.[9] Charles A. Coleman Jr. and William Marks, in their 1981 *History of Wind-Power on Martha's Vineyard*, described how these windmills worked:

"The typical sail works on Cape Cod and the Island consisted of a) one or more wind-powered pumps; b) a network of wooden pipes to carry the seawater from the pump to evaporation vats; and c) a wooden hood which was used to cover the vats during periods of heavy fog or rain. Because all of the components of the salt works are made from wood, there was only minor corrosion. The wooden vats and their wooden roofs, the wooden windmills, the wooden water pumps and pipes — they all had a very long life and required a minimum of maintenance."[10]

Coleman and Marks' research further revealed that by 1802, there were 136 separate salt producers generating more than 40,000 bushels of salt annually by employing this wind-based concept on Cape Cod and the islands. This number increased to 500 by 1861, capable of producing more than a million bushels of salt a year. Until the industry's demise by the early 1900s, "Hardly a town on the Cape and Islands was without one or more salt works complete with rows of windmills," they wrote.[11]

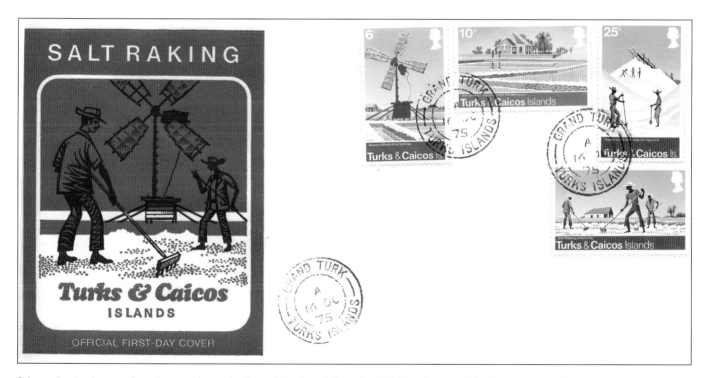

Salt production by use of small, portable windmills could be found along the U.S. East Coast and Caribbean in the 1800s and early 1900s. These 1975 postage stamps commemorate the salt industry's presence on the Turks & Caicos Islands.

It's unclear whether early windmills in the European style ever operated on the seas as floating structures. In 1594, Dutchman Cornelis Corneliszoon built a wind-driven sawmill. To sell the mill, it was constructed on a pontoon so that it could be easily moved from Amsterdam to Alkmaar. However, due to lack of interest, the pontoon with the mill was moved to Zaandam, where it was placed on-shore in 1596. No record exists that the windmill operated while on the pontoon. The long turning sails would have likely made the pontoon unstable.[12] In 1803, Napoleon Bonaparte proposed that his French army build windmills on pontoons in order to sustain an invasion of Britain. The idea was to build the structures in St. Malo, but the project was never carried out and the invasion was called off by the French in 1805.[13]

Some late nineteenth century sailing vessel operators deployed small windmills on their decks for mechanical and electric power generation. These floating windmills helped improve both operations and life aboard these ships, but in many cases were unreliable. Ships engaged in the Baltic timber trades often used windmills of multiple canvas sails constructed upon lattice towers to pump water by chain lift from deep inside their tightly packed vessel hulls. These windmills were sometimes referred to as "onkers," because of the "melancholy" sound they produced during operation.[14]

The sailing vessel *Chance*, a former man of war, merchant ship, and whaler, aground at Bluff, New Zealand in 1902. Note the vessel's deck-side wind-driven bilge pump.
Courtesy of the De Maus Collection, Alexander Turnbull Library, National Library of New Zealand, Wellington, New Zealand.

The distinctive steel and wood water-pumping American windmills first developed in the late nineteenth century also found their way onboard ships for bilge removal work. Prominent American windmill historian Dr. T. Lindsay Baker found during his research cases of ships with deck-side windmills engaged in the U.S. Pacific trades. For example, San Francisco, California-based windmill builder F. W. Krogh & Co. cited in its 1891 catalog two cases of its solid wheel wooden windmills being used on Scandinavian ships.[15] These windmills were still employed in the early twentieth century on a variety of ships, such as coal transporters, oil and ice barges, schooners, houseboats, and scows. A 1907 article by *The Industrial Magazine* described site and use of these windmills onboard these sailing ships:

> "A queer place for a windmill, which as everyone
> knows, is generally used for pumping water, is on board
> a vessel, but the Howell Bilge Pump Co., New York City,

In 1594, Dutchman Cornelis Corneliszoon built a wind-driven sawmill. It was constructed on a pontoon in Amsterdam for delivery to Alkmaar in the Netherlands. It's unclear whether the windmill operated while on the pontoon.

are supplying many sailing vessels with steel windmills for pumping out the overflow and leakage from the hold of the vessel.

"In a good many cases a pump is maintained on these vessels which is operated by gasoline, but the windmill pump obviates the handling of gasoline and requires no attention whatever. When in port the wheel may be started and as long as there is a breeze this will continue to operate automatically.

"The wheels are made self reefing and furling, which adds very materially in handling them at sea. They will pump from 1,500 to 15,000 gallons per day, according to the size of the windmill, and will operate with a four-mile breeze. The smallest size windmill is only four feet in diameter."[16]

A *Popular Mechanics* article from the time also discussed a patented windmill that could be placed on top of the vessel mast of schooners to avoid installing the windmill on deck and keeping it clear of the sail and boom.[17]

Unlike the bilge pumpers, onboard windmills for electric power carved themselves a more prominent place in maritime history. One of the earliest and most notable of these windmills was placed onboard the vessel *Fram*, which carried Norwegian scientist and explorer Fridtjof Nansen and his team from Christiana port in Norway to the Arctic in June 1893. The purpose of the three-year expedition was to test ice flows in the Arctic. When the *Fram* reached Cape Chelyuskin, the northern-most point of Siberia, it became held fast in the ice. The vessel's hull was specifically built to sustain the crushing pressure of the ice. Once in this position, the *Fram*'s crew erected a four-bladed windmill on the foredeck, which connected to a preinstalled dynamo just below deck. This windmill provided enough electricity to power a light in each crewman's cabin and the galley. It also powered a light on the outside of the vessel to serve as a beacon when Nansen and his crew ventured onto the ice to hunt and conduct scientific measurements. The windmill worked through the summer of 1895 when its main shaft broke beyond repair. The crew took it down and stowed it away. The *Fram* would break from the drifting ice pack in the spring of 1896 and sail back to Norway. The vessel remained active in Polar exploration, carrying Roald Amundsen on his expedition in 1910 to become the first person to reach the South Pole. Today, the ship serves as a museum in Oslo, Norway.[18]

The Norwegian polar vessel *Fram*, with its on-deck electric-generating windmill, stuck fast in the Arctic ice in 1893. The windmill operated through the summer of 1895 when the shaft to the generator snapped. *Courtesy of the Picture Collection, National Library of Norway, Oslo, Norway.*

Another well-known electric-generating windmill was placed on-board the wooden three-masted ship *Discovery*, which transported and served as a support base to British explorers Robert Falcon Scott and Ernest Shackleton at the South Pole in 1901 and 1904. The windmill was constructed by the Ontario Wind Engine & Pump Co. in Toronto, Canada, and shipped over to the East India Dock in London for installation on the foredeck of the *Discovery* just before its departure to Antarctica. The Canadian Airmotor, which had a traditional steel wind wheel design of an American water-pumping windmill, was connected to a dynamo under the deck to produce electric lighting.[19] The expedition vessel's chief engineer Reginald Skelton was not impressed by the Canadian Airmotor's durability, referring to it in his journal as "troublesome." He showed little remorse for the machine when it was eventually blown apart "to the relief of the engineering department."[20] The vessel now serves as a museum in Dundee harbor, Scotland, where it was built.

In May 1937, the Russians erected a floating electric-generating wind turbine of their own on a patch of ice in the North Pole to support a team of four scientists with basic lighting and power for radio communications to the outside world. The two-bladed Russian built turbine began producing electric power when the wind reached 7.7 yards per second and would shut off when it exceeded twenty-seven yards per second to avoid burning up the dynamo. Ivan Papanin, who headed the USSR Polar Drifting Expedition, wrote after his return from the nine-month expedition, "The wind motor charged our batteries unfailingly and we shall always think kindly of it for its good work." On June 18, 1937, Papanin wrote in his journal: "The wireless means life itself to us, and we value it especially highly, tending the instruments constantly and looking after the wind motor which faithfully charges our batteries."[21] Before departing the ice on February 19, 1938, Papanin added to his journal: "We must take (the wind motor) along when we are taken off this drifting floe. It ought to be kept on display in a museum. What a great help it has been to us! Better than anything else, it reflects the conditions and the way of life at the North Pole Drifting Station."[22]

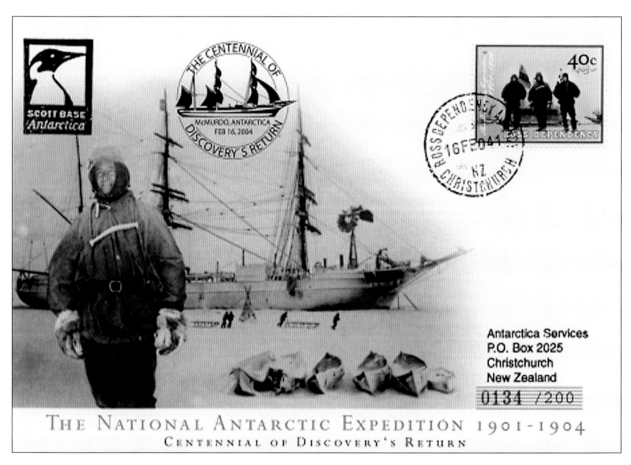

A New Zealand postal service postcard from February 2004 commemorating the 1901-1904 National Antarctic Expedition led by British explorers Robert Falcon Scott and Ernest Shackleton. On the deck of the vessel *Discovery*, an all-steel windmill built by the Ontario Wind Engine & Pump Co. of Toronto, Canada, met basic electricity needs during the expedition.

A Russian-built wind machine provided basic power to the Soviet Union's polar base weather and scientific station's radio equipment from May 1937 to February 1938. Photo taken July 5, 1937.

Chapter Two

Pioneers of Power

Coal had established itself as the primary energy source for the world's industrial centers by the late 1800s. However, scientists at the time wondered whether the world would run out of this precious energy source at the voluminous rate it was burning it. While we know now that there's still an abundance of coal, there was real concern then of a possible end to the supply, which meant the wheels of industry would come to a grinding halt, resulting in political and economic chaos of global proportion. Some inventive individuals at the time began to consider how the wind might serve as an electric power-generating source.

In 1881, Lord Kelvin, also known as Sir William Thomson, in a speech to the Mathematical and Physical Science of the British Association, hinted at the use of wind to generate electricity.[1] However, images of clunky old-style windmills and the dominant perception that the wind was an inconsistent force left many to wonder whether it could actually be considered a reliable source for generating electricity en masse.[2] There were those individuals with either private wealth or government-backing who were willing to give the wind a try. Two standouts during the late 1880s in the development of large early electric-generating windmills were American businessman and inventor Charles F. Brush and Danish mathematics and physics teacher Poul la Cour.

By the mid-1870s, Brush (1849-1929) was already well known for his work with the arc light and improvements made to the Gramme dynamo to support early electric lighting systems. He installed the first U.S. electric street lighting system in his hometown of Cleveland in 1879, and started the Brush Electric Company a year later. The company was also instrumental in developing more reliable batteries. In 1892, Brush's operation merged with Edison General Electric Company to become the General Electric Company.[3] In the winter of 1887-88, Brush pursued his quest for wind-generated electricity by constructing in his backyard what is believed to be the first automatically operated wind turbine for electric power generation. The windmill tower, rectangular in shape, stood about sixty feet tall and had a wind wheel spanning more than fifty-eight feet in diameter and made of 144 wooden rotor blades. Inside the windmill were a series of shafts, pulleys, and belts, which powered a dynamo. Brush maintained the windmill's electric output to

between seventy and seventy-five volts. The electricity was transmitted by wires to the basement of his house, which contained a bank of twelve batteries, each with thirty-four cells.[4] These batteries powered up to 350 incandescent lights throughout the house, in addition to two arc lights and three electric motors on the property. Brush's windmill successfully operated until 1909.

In 1891, La Cour (1846-1908) received 4,000 kroner from the Danish government to begin construction of his proposed electric generating windmills at the Askov Folk High School, where he taught. His goal was to use the electricity produced from two windmills to break down water into hydrogen and oxygen gas, which would further be stored in large containers and used for room lighting and heating. The experimental windmills allowed him to test curved sails to induce more electric output from the wind. La Cour was also credited with perpetuating interest in wind-generated electricity among engineers in the early 1900s. He formed the Danish Wind Electric Society (Dansk Vind Elektrisitets Selskab) in 1905. Under La Cour's stewardship, the organization had more than 350 members and published the world's first journal dedicated to wind power.[5]

Yet the idea of using large-scale wind turbine technology near shore or on the ocean surface itself was largely unconsidered by wind energy proponents at the time. In 1907, Reginald Aubrey Fessenden (1866-1932), a Canadian born radio pioneer who at one point worked in the laboratory of Thomas Edison, filed for a patent in 1907 with a technique aimed at providing a system for storing solar-generated power. In his patent application, Fessenden wrote:

"The invention herein described relates to the utilization of intermittent sources of power and more particularly to natural intermittent sources, such as solar radiation and wind power, and has for its object the efficient and practical storage of power so derived. It has long been recognized that mankind must, in the near future, be faced by a shortage of power unless some means were devised for storing power derived from the intermittent sources of nature. These sources are, however, intermittent and the problem of storing them in a practicable way, i.e. at a cost which should be less than that of direct generation from coal, has for many years engaged the attention of the most eminent engineers, among whom may be mentioned Edison, Lord Kelvin, Ayrton, Perry, and Brush..."[6]

In a paper presented to the British Association in late 1910, Fessenden proposed the installation of a solar system to heat water at sea-level and pipe the steam up a cliff-side to a reservoir where it cooled and condensed back to water. The water in the reservoir would then be returned over the cliff where at the bottom it would turn an electric dynamo. A group of wind turbines mounted to a large steel rotating array would provide electric power at night when the solar system is at rest. However, the *Scientific American* editors in an article at the time expressed a degree of skepticism about the practically of Fessenden's proposed system.[7]

Shortly after World War I, the ideas for utility-scale electric-generating windmills proliferated, especially among European and Russian engineers. Proposed land-based giants included both single and multiple rotors on top of large steel lattice structures that resembled a version of the Eiffel Tower. These wind turbine designs pushed the bounds of engineering with their extreme heights, amounts of required metals, and large moving rotor systems. In the 1920s, two German engineers grabbed the public's attention with their theoretic contributions to big wind power.

This is a 1907 illustration of Reginald Aubrey Fessenden's patent, which proposed a combination of near-shore wind and solar for large-scale power storage.

As a young man, Anton Flettner (1885-1961) became interested in the design and uses of rotors. In 1924, he oversaw the construction of a wind-powered electric rotor ship. A former schooner was fitted with two tall cylindrical rotors, which drove an electric propulsion system, using the so-called Magnus effect. The Magnus effect, named for German physicist Heinrich Magnus who described it in 1852, is the force acting on a perpendicular spinning body in a moving airstream. Flettner's vessel, *Baden-Baden*, successfully crossed the Atlantic, arriving in New York Harbor in 1926 using the Magnus effect from the wind.[8]

Flettner continued his research of rotor-based wind turbines through a syndicate of German firms named the Flettner Windturbine Company. The company built its first four-blade 66-foot diameter wind wheel on top of a 160-foot steel tower. In his 1926 book *Mein Weg zum Rotor*, Flettner asserts, "This windmill is only intended as the first link in the development of our large wheels. We begin about with the size where the windmill builders heretofore have stopped, but next year we intend to develop the giant windmill using wheels of 300 ft. diameter and over."[9] He proposed wind turbines with towers more than six hundred

German engineer Anton Flettner, the father of the helicopter, experimented with wind-powered electric rotor ships during the 1920s.

Flettner drew inspiration for his electric rotor ship from earlier proposed mechanical designs such as Du Quet's 1712 windpower ship and Constantin's repeller boat *Bois-Rosé* in 1924.

feet high with 300-foot diameter wind wheels mounted with smaller high-speed propellers on the tip of each rotor blade. Of this idea, Flettner wrote:

"When the main wheel is revolving, the extreme tips of the wings move through the air at a velocity which amounts to several times, say four times, the velocity of the wind blowing at the particular time. At a wind of 16 m.p.h., the tip in this case has a velocity 64 m.p.h. If a person imagined himself placed at the extreme end of the rotor, he would be in a 'rotation wind' of 64 m.p.h. From this rotation wind one can abstract by a machine of equal power 4 x 4 x 4 — 64 times as much energy than from the 'natural' wind which drives the main wheel. Hence if we arrange for four secondary wheels, each of these secondary wheels can be given an area of one 256th of the main wheel."[10]

Flettner's electric rotor ship *Baden-Baden* starting its voyage to the United States in 1925.

Wind-Propeller Sails Proposed For Liners

Air blast from fan turns windmill mounted on model boat, in demonstration at English inventor's exhibit. At right is artist's conception of ocean liner using the wind-propeller sails.

Wind-generated electric propulsion for ocean-going vessels continued until World War II. A 1935 *Modern Mechanix* article outlined an English patent for a vessel with a giant wind wheel that would replace the power of a traditional below-deck steam engine.

However, Flettner discontinued his wind turbine work at the start of World War II and focused on the development, for which now he is better known, of rotor-based vertical lift aircraft, or helicopters, first for the German military and later for the U.S. government.

In the mid-1920s, the Flettner Windturbine Company in Germany constructed a land-based electric-generating wind turbine with a 66-foot diameter wind wheel, with the intention of designing turbines with wheels three hundred feet in diameter.

German inventor Hermann Honnef (1878-1961) also fostered world interest in colossal electric-producing wind turbines in the years leading up to World War II. On a large concrete base, Honnef proposed to build a wind tower of welded lightweight steel tubes to a height of 1,500 feet. At more than 1,000 feet off the ground, Honnef found that the wind's speed consistently remained above 10 mph. His proposed giant turbine consisted of three to five double rotors each with a diameter of up to 250 feet, which Honnef claimed could generate fifty megawatts of power annually.[11] Taking into account the potential for damage to the wind wheels by gale-force winds, the top of the tower included a rolling platform, called a bascule, which would in effect tilt the wind wheels toward a horizontal position to reduce their contact with the wind.[12]

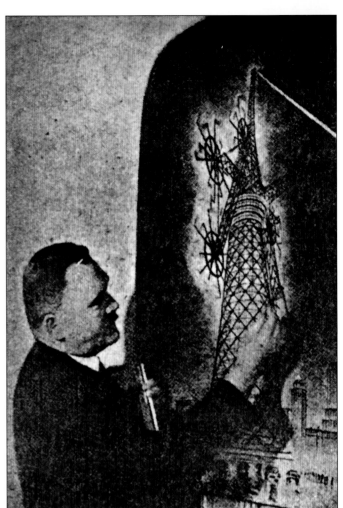

In 1929, German engineer Hermann Honnef presented his wind turbine design that featured five sets of blades and a capacity of 100,000 kilowatts. *Courtesy of the Archives, Bad Honnef, Germany.*

Right:
A sensational illustration on the cover of the September 3, 1938 *Modern Wonder* issue depicts Honnef's giant wind turbines.

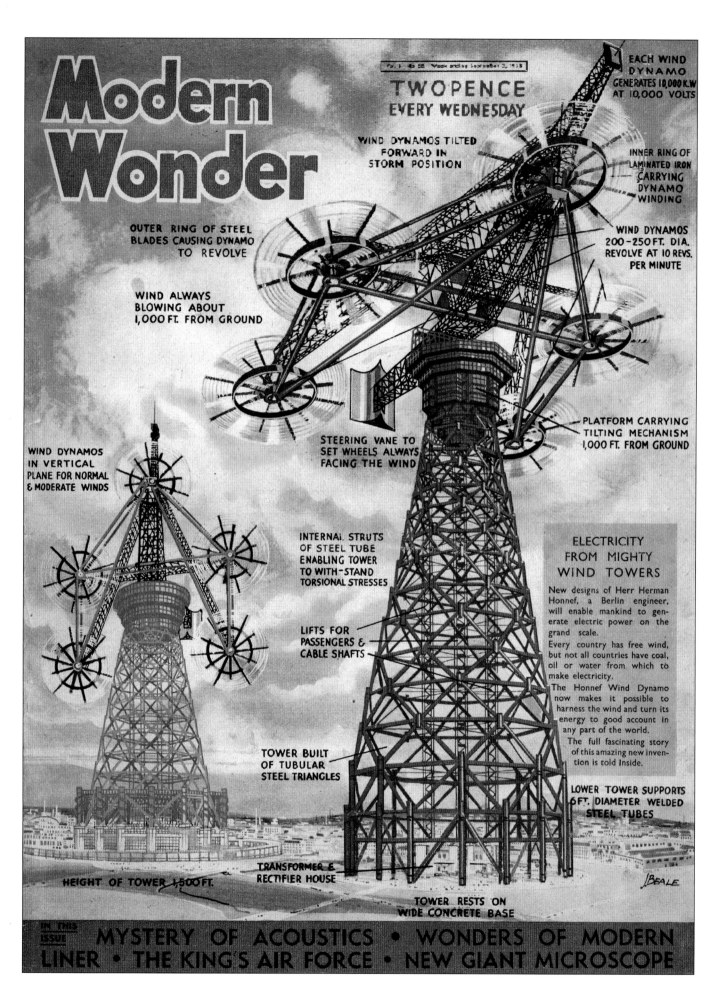

Modern Wonder

TWOPENCE
EVERY WEDNESDAY

EACH WIND DYNAMO GENERATES 10,000 K.W AT 10,000 VOLTS

WIND DYNAMOS TILTED FORWARD IN STORM POSITION

INNER RING OF LAMINATED IRON CARRYING DYNAMO WINDING

OUTER RING OF STEEL BLADES CAUSING DYNAMO TO REVOLVE

WIND DYNAMOS 200-250 FT. DIA. REVOLVE AT 10 REVS. PER MINUTE

WIND ALWAYS BLOWING ABOUT 1,000 FT. FROM GROUND

PLATFORM CARRYING TILTING MECHANISM 1,000 FT. FROM GROUND

STEERING VANE TO SET WHEELS ALWAYS FACING THE WIND

WIND DYNAMOS IN VERTICAL PLANE FOR NORMAL & MODERATE WINDS

INTERNAL STRUTS OF STEEL TUBE ENABLING TOWER TO WITH-STAND TORSIONAL STRESSES

ELECTRICITY FROM MIGHTY WIND TOWERS

New designs of Herr Herman Honnef, a Berlin engineer, will enable mankind to generate electric power on the grand scale.

Every country has free wind, but not all countries have coal, oil or water from which to make electricity.

The Honnef Wind Dynamo now makes it possible to harness the wind and turn its energy to good account in any part of the world.

The full fascinating story of this amazing new invention is told inside.

LIFTS FOR PASSENGERS & CABLE SHAFTS

LOWER TOWER SUPPORTS 6 FT. DIAMETER WELDED STEEL TUBES

TOWER BUILT OF TUBULAR STEEL TRIANGLES

HEIGHT OF TOWER 1,500 FT.

TRANSFORMER & RECTIFIER HOUSE

TOWER RESTS ON WIDE CONCRETE BASE

J.BEALE

Honnef is considered by wind industry historians to be the first to propose a large-scale offshore wind turbine. In his 1932 book *Windkraftwerke*, Honnef described an offshore double-rotor system similar to that of his onshore design. The wind wheel was 160 meters (525 feet) in diameter with an annual output of twenty megawatts based on an average wind speed of fifteen meters per second (33 mph). The concept never made it off paper, and the rotor design was later found to be technically unfeasible.[13]

In 1941, Honnef was picked by the German Reich to manage a small wind energy program. On Mathias Hill in Bötzow, Germany, he tested double-rotor wind turbines with wheel diameters of 10 meters (thirty-three feet). Later studies showed that a double-rotor produces only five percent more power than a single rotor and cost twice the amount to construct compared to a single rotor wheel. The largest wind plant on the Mathias Hill test field during the war had a capacity of 15 kilowatts. The tests stopped by the war's end and the turbines were dismantled. For his achievements in windpower generation, Honnef was awarded the Order of Merit of the Federal Republic of Germany on July 16, 1952.[14]

A more successful large land-based wind turbine test was conducted during World War II by American Palmer Cosslett Putnam, a one-time geologist, flyer for Britain during World War I, and former president of New York publisher G. P. Putnam's Sons. With cooperation from General Electric, water turbine maker S. Morgan Smith Company, and the New England Public Service Company, which provided the test site, Putnam was able to pursue his plans to build the turbine even in the face of the United States entering the war.[15]

In the summer of 1941, work started in earnest on the turbine on Grandpa's Knob, a 2,000-foot summit located between Castleton and West Rutland, Vermont. Putnam's turbine weighed about 240 tons and included a 110-foot steel tower with a 36-foot square base anchored to four concrete pilings set into the mountain. The two turbine blades were shot-welded stainless steel, measuring sixty-five feet long and eleven feet wide, and weighed about 15,300 pounds each. The turbine's generator was rated at 1,250 kilowatts. The power was fed to the Central Vermont Public Service Corporation. Putnam's turbine was considered the first attempt to leverage windpower to feed alternating current into an existing power grid.[16] Despite setbacks from bearing and blade damage between February 1943 and March 1945, Putnam's turbine experiment was considered a success and generated worldwide interest.[17]

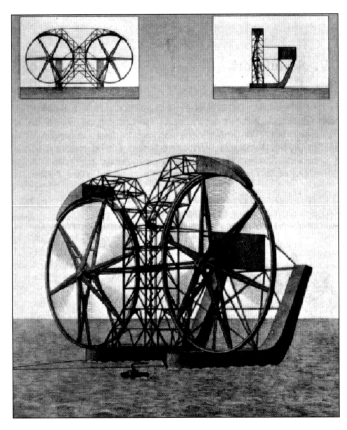

In his 1932 book, *Windkraftwerke*, Honnef proposed a design for a large offshore wind turbine. The double-rotor concept was deemed technically unfeasible.

Palmer Cosslett Putnam's 1,250-kilowatt utility-scale turbine was erected at Grandpa's Knob, Vermont, in 1941.

Denmark also remained active in wind energy during World War II. Under the control of the German Reich, Danish engineering firm F. L. Smidth (today a construction products maker) built a number of two-bladed and three-bladed wind turbines, rated between sixty and seventy kilowatts each. The blades of the F. L. Smidth turbines were made of wood that was coated with special paints to make it weatherproof, while the wind-facing side of the blades was reinforced with special metal fittings.[18] The two-bladed turbine had a rotor diameter of fifty-seven feet, and the three-bladed turbine had a rotor diameter of seventy-nine feet.[19]

The early wind turbine towers were made of either metal or concrete. However, the shortage of metal in Denmark during the war resulted in the majority of towers being made of concrete, a specialty of F. L. Smidth. An advantage of concrete towers was the lower maintenance compared to the metal construction, which required regular renewal of protective coatings.[20] The F. L. Smidth turbines started to feed electricity into an accumulator for grid connection when the wind speed reached five meters per second. The nominal capacity was 50 kilowatts at ten meters per second (22 mph).[21] During the development of these turbines, one of F. L. Smidth's two-bladed turbines installed at Gedser Harbor became the first functional "offshore" electric-generating wind turbine, although its tower was accessible from shore by an elevated gangway.

During World War II, the Danish engineering firm F. L. Smidth (now a cement machinery manufacturer) built this two-bladed wind machine at Gedser Harbor. It's considered by many historians to be the first functional "offshore" electric-generating wind turbine. *Courtesy of F. L. Smidth & Co. A/S, Valby, Denmark.*

In 1946, Percy H. Thomas, an engineer with the United States Federal Power Commission, designed a 475-foot tower topped by two large rotors, each with a 200-foot diameter and capable together of generating 7,500 kilowatts. These generators would be mounted on a large turntable that also housed the generating equipment.[22] Thomas proposed erecting these massive turbines in groups around the country to supplement hydroelectric and coal-fired power plants. He received support for his idea within the federal government and a bill was written by Congress to begin construction on one of the turbines. However, lawmakers dropped the proposal at the start of the Korean War in 1951.[23]

From the early 1950s to the mid-1960s, large wind turbine tests carried out in Denmark, Great Britain, France, and Germany remained land-based and highly experimental. Wind turbine-produced power simply had a difficult time competing with traditional power sources, such as coal and petroleum, and the proliferation of nuclear power plants. It wasn't until the 1973 Arab oil embargo that interest in large-scale wind turbine technology would reemerge. Many countries would establish government-supported alternative energy research programs throughout the early 1970s.

In 1946, U.S. Federal Power Commission engineer Percy H. Thomas proposed a wind turbine with a 475-foot tower topped by two large rotors, each with a 200-foot diameter and capable of generating 7,500 kilowatts.

In 1956-57, Danish engineer Johannes Juul designed and oversaw construction of this three-bladed, 200-kilowatt turbine at Gedser, Denmark, which inspired other developers.

In 1976, the Danish government set up an ambitious long-term energy independence program that encouraged development of wind turbines and offshore natural gas exploration. The scientists and engineers at the country's Risø National Laboratory studied various designs of large-scale turbines with the intent to offer the research to the commercial sector. In 1980, Bonus Energy (now Siemens) built a popular 30-kilowatt machine. Other notable Danish manufacturers, such as Vestas and NEG Micon, expanded their role in the wind turbine business in the mid- to late 1980s. The Danish government also established regulations to feed wind-generated electricity into the national power grid.[24] The U.S. government implemented a wind energy program of its own under the jurisdiction of the National Science Foundation (shortly absorbed into the Energy Research and Development Administration and rolled into the newly formed Department of Energy in 1977). The foundation, in turn, handed the program over in late 1973 to the engineers at the National Aeronautics and Space Administration (NASA) Lewis Research Center in Cleveland, Ohio.[25]

Some scientists and engineers believed that land-based wind turbines could only nibble at the edges of society's ever-increasing electrical energy needs, and without the ability to generate voluminous power would never be able to compete with the likes of fossil or nuclear fuels. They also noted that society's tolerance for wind turbines would become increasingly strained as their numbers sprouted upon the landscape. In addition, geographic constraints and available winds limit the land sites suitable for wind farm development. Less land availability in Europe resulted in many wind turbines being erected in people's backyards. In North America, the windiest sites are in sparsely populated areas, such as the Upper Midwest and West Texas, requiring webs of costly and unsightly transmission lines to get the electric power over long distances to where it's most needed.

William E. Heronemus (1920-2002), a former Navy captain and professor at the University of Massachusetts at Amherst, stunned a Senate subcommittee in 1973 by stating that the entire United States could power itself from solar energy, which by definition included windpower, by the year 2000.[26] At the time, the United States and the rest of the world was reeling from the Arab oil embargo. Some suggested breaking the country's oil dependence by developing more nuclear power plants, of which Heronemus was firmly opposed. "The entire concept of a plutonium economy is insane… The idea that the most toxic material in the face of the earth should be used to provide energy for humanity is one of the most absurd ideas of all time," he warned.[27] Heronemus had worked with nuclear power in the Navy and was well aware of its dangers. By 1972, he had founded the Wind Power Group in the UMass Engineering Department, with a focus on offshore windpower and ocean thermal energy. This became his platform to design some of the most inspiring offshore wind energy concepts in the history of the technology.

In 1973, William E. Heronemus, a former Navy captain and professor at the University of Massachusetts at Amherst, stunned a U.S. Senate subcommittee by stating that the entire United States could power itself by solar energy, including windpower, by the year 2000.
Courtesy of Marcia Heronemus-Pate, Tulsa, Oklahoma.

Heronemus gathered inspiration from earlier large-scale wind plant developers and thinkers, such as Putnam, Thomas, and Edward William Golding, who wrote and published the influential book *The Generation of Electricity by Wind Power* in 1955.[28] Unlike his predecessors, Heronemus understood that the most useful winds for power generation weren't on land, but on the sea. In a paper to the Marine Technology Society in 1972, Heronomus stated: "It is suggested that man might once again turn to those mighty winds and to ocean currents… to help satisfy his need for energy. If such energy were used, it would be essentially pollution-free and would have a neutral effect on global heating."[29] He then proceeded to lay out his plan for the Offshore Wind Power System (OWPS), which consisted of a network of more than 160 floating wind generators off the coast of New England. Each unit, consisting of three 200-foot diameter two-bladed rotors, would be capable of generating up to 6 megawatts. This electricity would be fed by underwater cables to a manned offshore "electrolyzer" plant, which would extract hydrogen from the seawater. The liquid hydrogen would be stored in deep-water tanks and pumped to shore by pipeline to produce electricity for fuel cells.[30] He estimated that the system at full production could produce nine to ten times the amount of power used at that time by the six-state region.[31] Ever cognizant of the environmental impact, he noted that the closest turbines would be at least ten miles off Cape Cod, Massachusetts, "far enough to prevent visual pollution."[32] He even suggested that the concept was equally applicable for offshore wind projects in the Great Lakes.[33]

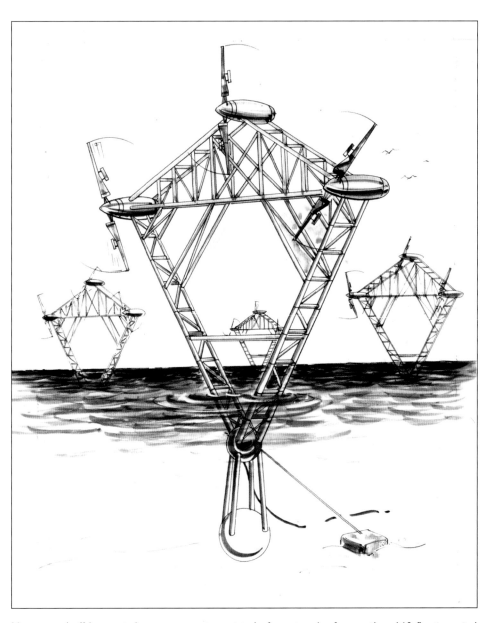

Heronemus' offshore windpower concept consisted of a network of more than 160 floating wind turbine generators off the coast of New England. Each unit, consisting of three 200-foot diameter two-bladed rotors, would generate up to 6 megawatts.
Courtesy of Marcia Heronemus-Pate, Tulsa, Oklahoma.

The OWPS concept captured the imagination of the general public and was widely reported by the press, such as the *New York Times* and *National Geographic*, in the early 1970s. Heronemus was both praised and ridiculed for his ideas. He was also not afraid to speak out against his opponents, once telling an interviewer: "In sum, those learned members of our Great Society who publish such tripe as 'Wind is for the birds' on the front page of the *New York Times* are simply demonstrating their ignorance... toward that which really is a key to energy, prosperity, and improved quality of life in the future."[34]

There were certainly those influential Capitol Hill lawmakers and energy policy makers at the time who were inspired by Heronemus' work. In the energy budget for fiscal year 1976, Massachusetts Sen. Ted Kennedy, later to become an ardent opponent of a wind farm off the coast of Cape Cod (see *Chapter 9*), introduced an offshore windpower amendment, which required the federal government to conduct a feasibility study and report its findings back to Congress in a future budget request for a megawatt-scale offshore windpower demonstration project.[35] The Energy Research and Development Administration subsequently provided funds to Westinghouse and General Electric to study the concept.[36] Professor David Rittenhouse Inglis, a colleague of Heronemus at UMass, in a 1978 article called the government's attempt at testing OWPS "dilatory," stating that "An industrial giant with competing vested interests might yield to a bias toward an unfavorable result, while an independent group of able engineers might be more apt to finding ways to make the proposal feasible... As it was, the sole offshore-feasibility contract (for almost a quarter of million dollars) was awarded to the firm most heavily involved in nuclear energy, Westinghouse."[37]

That year the Carter administration put its backing largely behind solar energy and a policy decision within the Energy Department concluded that "offshore is out" because it was economically unfeasible.[38]

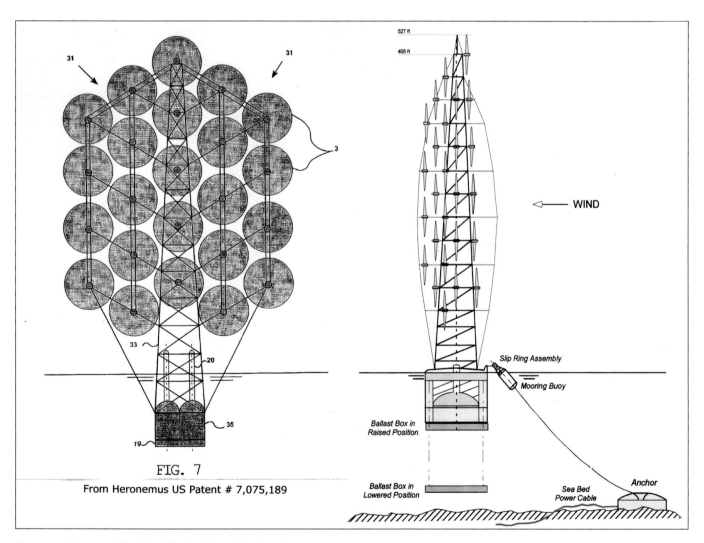

FIG. 7

From Heronemus US Patent # 7,075,189

Heronemus' proposed "wind sail" included a multitude of rotors per tower.
Courtesy of Marcia Heronemus-Pate, Tulsa, Oklahoma.

The U.S. government focused its testing on large-scale land-based wind turbines. NASA built its first wind turbine at the Plum Brook Test Station near Sandusky, Ohio in 1975. The turbine, known as Mod-0, was constructed on a four-legged 100-foot tall truss tower and included a two-bladed rotor with a 125-foot diameter. NASA believed the two-blade turbine was more economical to build than a three-blade unit and yet just as efficient. The Mod-0 produced 100 kilowatts of power in 18-mph winds. Wind direction was sensed by a vane on top of the gearbox and monitored by an automatic yaw control system.[39]

The turbine allowed NASA to test many aspects of wind turbine design and build even larger test models. These experimental turbines were built throughout the U.S. continent, Hawaii and Puerto Rico. While sticking with the two-blade concept, NASA's turbines became larger both in size and output. In 1987, the agency, together with Boeing, completed construction of its largest turbine, the Mod-5B at Oahu, Hawaii on July 1, 1987. The unit consistently produced 3.2 megawatts of power in winds ranging from 13 to 17 mph.[40]

NASA continued its wind energy program through the mid-1980s when the Reagan administration cut its funding. The price per barrel of oil at the time had dropped significantly, undermining the economic benefits of renewable energy sources in the eyes of the U.S. government. The initial Mod-0 wind turbine was dismantled in February 1987, and the last of the NASA-inspired turbines disappeared from the landscape by the mid-1990s. Other U.S. government agencies had their own wind energy programs during the mid-1970s and early 1980s, including Sandia National Laboratories in Albuquerque, New Mexico, and Department of Agriculture's Bushland, Texas facility, which focused on the development of the large-scale Darrieus vertical axis turbines that resembled giant upside down eggbeaters. A 122-foot model with a 165-foot vertical tower was erected at Bushland for testing in 1988. The model produced 500 kilowatts of power in winds ranging from 25 to 40 mph. Similar to NASA, these programs' output waxed and waned with the availability for congressional appropriations.

Here again, Heronemus is considered to have outdone the existing government wind energy programs at the time. In the mid-1970s, he and his team of engineering students constructed a 25-kilowatt wind turbine on the UMass campus. The turbine, called the WF-1, had three fiberglass pitch-regulated blades with a rotor diameter of 32.5 feet. The rotor turned at variable speed, and had a near constant tip speed ratio so that it was efficient across a range of wind speeds. The turbine was also computer controlled. Most of WF-1's operational aspects have since been incorporated in today's modern turbines.[41] The machine became the forerunner to the turbines built by U.S. Windpower — arguably the first American manufacturer of utility-scale turbines — in the early 1980s. U.S. Windpower went on to become Kennetech, which was later acquired by Enron and then by GE Wind. The turbine, which was dismantled in 2004 for preservation, also served as a training station for Heronemus' students, many of whom have contributed significantly to the research and development of wind energy technology during the past thirty years.[42]

Heronemus, often dubbed the "Wind King" and the "father of modern windpower," left UMass in the 1980s. He returned twice as needed as a part-time professor and formed his own wind energy firm. In 1998, Heronemus incorporated his sole proprietorship to form Ocean Wind Energy Systems Inc. with former student Woody Stoddard to continue work on his multi-rotor wind turbine array wind ships. (His daughter Marcia Heronemus-Pate now heads the company.) In 1999, the American Wind Energy Association presented Heronemus its Lifetime Achievement Award "in recognition of the inspiration that he provided to a generation of wind energy engineers and of a vision for the wind industry that is only now starting to be realized."[43]

Indeed, many of his UMass engineering students went on to form their own wind energy companies or become key staff to federal energy agencies, such as the National Renewable Energy Laboratory. Before his death, Heronemus also had the satisfaction of witnessing the first offshore wind farms being erected in the seas of Northern Europe.

Right:
In 1975, NASA built its first full-scale 100-kilowatt test wind turbine, known as Mod-0, at the Lewis Plum Brook Test Station near Sandusky, Ohio. *Courtesy of the NASA Glenn Research Center, Cleveland, Ohio.*

41

Chapter Three

Moving Offshore

Several Northern European countries and wind equipment manufacturers in the mid-1970s and 1980s began to study the feasibility of erecting turbines in coastal waters. The leap from land to sea appeared to be the most logical step forward in the development of utility-grade wind power generation, a key component for how many of these countries hoped to break their near complete dependence on imported fossil fuels. Yet, these engineers faced a myriad of technical challenges for how to successfully take land-based turbine technology and introduce it to the harsh marine environment. It required the creation of new approaches and supporting equipment for turbine installation and maintenance processes. While the North Sea's well-developed offshore oil and gas industry served as a model for moving wind farms out to sea, the wind turbines on the drawing boards had their own structural and performance attributes that set them apart. Early offshore wind studies also focused on perspective projects located over 10 kilometers from shore and capable of generating more than 100 megawatts of power. Although no turbines were constructed during this period, this work served as the foundation for the first offshore wind farms.[1]

Dr. Peter Musgrove, an engineer and expert on wind energy, proposed in 1976 that the United Kingdom should take advantage of its strong coastal winds by building groups of turbines offshore, particularly in the southern North Sea in the shallow waters off the Wash. He suggested building a series of 1,000-megawatt offshore wind farms, each consisting of four hundred 2.5-megawatt turbines. Unlike the floating offshore wind farm proposals made at the time by Professor William Heronemus, an American engineer, Musgrove favored erecting these wind turbines on foundations directly attached to the seabed as the most economic and technically feasible way forward.[2]

Musgrove soon won over skeptics in the British government. In 1978, the Department of Energy and Central Electricity Generating Board completed a joint offshore site study, which concluded that there were no significant obstacles to placing wind turbines offshore. A second, more detailed study finished in 1982 showed that the United Kingdom's offshore wind potential was nearly equal to 230 terawatt hours, or the total country's electric supply at the time.[3]

In 1976, Peter Musgrove, an engineer specializing in wind energy, urged the British government to take advantage of its strong coastal winds for the production of electricity.

By the late 1980s, the Department of Energy and Central Electricity Generating Board had developed plans to acquire a 750-kilowatt turbine from turbine manufacturer James Howden Ltd. and erect it about 5 kilometers (three miles) off Wells-Next-The-Sea and connect it to the Eastern Electricity Board's system onshore, conceivably making it the first European country to witness the installation of an offshore wind turbine. However, in 1989, the project unraveled when Howden abruptly left the wind energy business due to financial reasons and technical troubles associated with its smaller landside turbines in California.[4] While there wasn't a race to be the first European country to take wind energy development to the ocean, the honor would technically fall to Sweden.

Sweden had been involved in windpower since 1975 as a reaction to the oil crisis and hazardous waste stigma associated with nuclear energy. At the time, the Swedish public in general was critical of the one-sided drive for nuclear power and wanted renewable alternatives to imported fossil fuels. In 1979, the country undertook the decision to build two large wind turbines, two and three megawatts respectively. The 3-megawatt unit, which was developed jointly by Karlskronavarvet (belonging to Swedeyards, the state-owned company that had taken over the shipbuilding industry at the time of the crisis) and U.S. firm Hamilton Standard was installed at Maglarp in southern Sweden in 1982. It was considered one of the most successful of its time. The machine operated with only minor technical problems until its demolition in 1992. Also during this period, the province of Blekinge in southern Sweden had promoted the development of a large offshore wind project.

The studies were conducted mainly by Rune Hardell and Bo Björk of consulting firm Energia together with VBB, a large Swedish civil engineering consultancy (now part of Sweco). The result was the development of a tripod design to attach the wind turbine base to the seafloor. Swedish Shipyards was picked to manufacture the tripod base. The designers also settled on the use of a 220-kilowatt turbine developed by Danish WindWorld (later acquired by NEG Micon and finally Vestas). The 27-ton unit had a rotor diameter of 25 meters (82 feet) and a hub height from the wind turbine tower base of 37.5 meters (123 feet). Sven Thörnqvist, development director of Sydkraft, then the second largest electric utility in Sweden (now part of Germany's Eon), oversaw the management of the turbine's construction. During the system's development, program manager Staffan Engström of Statens Energiverk (National Energy Administration) is credited with proposing the combination of offshore application and the novel foundation design with the proven WindWorld turbine. The result was a turn-key delivery by Swedish construction company BPA Bygg AB.[5]

In the late 1980s, the British government planned to acquire a 750-kilowatt turbine from manufacturer James Howden Ltd. and erect it about five kilometers off Wells-Next-The-Sea. The plan was scrapped in 1989 when Howden ran into financial and technical problems.

The turbine installation, named "Svante I" after Svante Ingemarsson, the county administrator who supported the project, was installed at a site about 250 meters (273 yards) from the shore at Nogersund, a village in the southeastern part of Sweden facing the Baltic Sea, at a water depth of 6 meters (twenty feet). During the summer of 1990, the complete installation was floated by barge from Karlskronavarvet, about sixty miles along the coast, to the site where it was eased onto a level gravel bed and secured. First connection to the landside power grid was made September 25, 1990. However, problems with the connecting power cable delayed the formal delivery. Studies conducted on the wind turbine's impact on local bird and fish populations were found to be minimal.[6]

Already in 1991, parts of the steel frame base appeared corroded, although it was believed that the Corten steel was supposed to be resistant to corrosion. Three years later, the turbine was destroyed by fire and a new machine of the same type was installed on the foundation. The fire started in the generator, the most common cause of total failure and mostly the result of electric faults and lightning strikes. The turbine remained in service until November 2004, generating about 369-megawatt hours a year. During its years in operation, the world's first modern offshore wind turbine had become a matter of pride for many locals who opposed its dismantling in June 2007 and favored its continued operation.[7]

In 1991, Denmark became the first country to string together a series of turbines in the sea to create the world's first offshore wind farm. By the end of the 1980s, the country had already installed numerous land-based wind turbines. Their presence began to split the population between those who supported and those who opposed more land-based turbine construction. It thus became necessary for Denmark to explore alternatives for expanding its wind energy. It was estimated that an offshore wind farm should produce sixty to seventy percent more electric power than land-based turbines due to the unobstructed access to stronger ocean winds.[8]

The first modern offshore wind turbine, a 220-kilowatt WindWorld unit, started sending power to shore on September 25, 1990. *Courtesy of Staffan Engström, Lidingö, Sweden.*

The planning for Denmark's first offshore wind farm took several years. In November 1987, the Danish Energy Ministry together with ELSAM and ELKRAFT, the country's two main groupings of electric power producers and distributing companies, and DEF (the Association of Danish Electrical Producing Companies) formed the Committee for Offshore Windfarms. The committee's role was to point out one or two locations for the offshore demonstration projects. A technical working group within the committee studied various foundation types, seawater depths, seabed conditions, and offshore wind resources. The committee ultimately determined that a placement in the Baltic Sea north of the village of Vindeby on the island of Lolland was most convenient. Lolland consisted mostly of farmland and the distance to the nearest city was about twenty kilometers. Most farmers in the area had their own wind turbines and were generally not opposed to the offshore wind farm project.[9]

Since the offshore site was located in the eastern part of Denmark, Elkraft (later split into Dong Energy and Energinet.dk) became the leader of the project. Elkraft named Frank Olsen project manager and he was in charge of the project in cooperation with the utility company SEAS (now SEAS-NVE). Numerous consultants and specialist engineering firms were gathered to assist with the project. Early on, it was determined that the wind farm would use eleven 450 kilowatt-rated Bonus Wind Systems turbines.[10] Each turbine consisted of three 16-meter (52-foot) blades made of polyester reinforced with glass fiber, attached to the top of a 35-meter (115-foot) tall steel tubular tower.[11] These turbines included extra room for high voltage transformers inside the turbine towers, entrance doors located at a height above the splash zone, and onboard winches for lifting large components.

Looking down from a platform onto the maintenance vessel at the base of the world's first modern offshore turbine at Nogersund, Sweden. *Courtesy of Staffan Engström, Lidingö, Sweden.*

N&R Groner was employed to design the foundations based on:

- Size and load of the turbines.
- Water depths of 2.5 to 8 meters (eight to twenty-six feet) at the site.
- Seabed conditions (consisting mostly of hard clay covered with a 20 to 30 centimeter (8 to 12 inch) layer of fine sand).
- Minimizing impact on fishing activities.[12]

It was determined that Monberg & Thorsen would cast the eleven 8-meter (26 feet) tall concrete foundations at a nearby dry dock, and once cured, Jensen & Christensen would install them at the offshore site 300 meters (328 yards) apart and in two even rows separated by 300 meters (328 yards). The foundations were filled with gravel for weighting them to the seafloor and surrounded with large boulders to prevent current erosion. ELKRAFT hired the firm Em. Z. Svitzer to install the turbines on the foundations. Svitzer used two pontoons and two tugboats for the turbine installations.

Seabed foundations for the Vindeby wind turbines were constructed in a dyke enclosure near the town of Onsevig, Denmark.
Courtesy of SEAS-NVE Holding A/S, Haslev, Denmark.

A pontoon is used to lift the Vindeby wind turbine foundations from the
casting area to the site near Lolland, Denmark.
Courtesy of SEAS-NVE Holding A/S, Haslev, Denmark.

A trencher is used to bury underwater cables between the
Vindeby wind turbines into the seabed.
Courtesy of SEAS-NVE Holding A/S, Haslev, Denmark.

Installation of electrical components for the 450-kilowatt Bonus Wind Systems turbines at Vindeby.
Courtesy of SEAS-NVE Holding A/S, Haslev, Denmark.

One pontoon carried the turbines and the other carried the installation crane. NKT Engineering was contracted to supply and lay the 17.5-kilovolt submarine cables. The cables included optical fibers to allow for electronic monitoring of the turbines' performance from shore. Dansk Dykker Enterprise was used to bury the submarine cables into the seabed after their laying. The company also installed the dry transformers and GIS-switchgear for the wind turbines supplied by ABB Electric.[13]

The Vindeby offshore wind farm was activated in 1991 with no immediate breakdowns or glitches. Only a few minor adjustments to the control and measuring systems in the turbines had to be made during the first few weeks of operation. In subsequent years, the wind farm has performed well. Some of the turbines required worn gearbox bearings to be replaced, but nothing more significant. The landing stages placed on the foundations had to be changed several times during the winter since floating ice destroyed them. The cone-shaped turbine foundations at Vindeby are smallest at the top, whereas newer concrete foundations are biggest at the top. This gives a better landing stage for technicians and equipment, and floating ice cannot destroy them.[14] Since it was the first offshore wind farm, Vindeby has been one of the most heavily monitored sites. Two anemometer masts were installed at the site to study wind conditions and turbulence. Denmark's Risø National Laboratory has used the data collected by the anemometer masts to support a number of wind energy studies. These studies have found that Vindeby's electricity production is about twenty percent higher than on comparable land sites, however production is somewhat reduced by wind "shade" from the island of Lolland.[15]

The 11-turbine Vindeby offshore wind farm was activated in 1991 with no immediate breakdowns or glitches.
Courtesy of SEAS-NVE Holding A/S, Haslev, Denmark.

Despite the success at Vindeby, offshore wind farm developments in Europe remained modest through the rest of the century. Much of the continent's focus on wind energy exploitation continued on land. The next offshore wind farm was erected off the coast of the Netherlands at Lely (Ijsselmeer) in 1994 and included four NedWind 500-kilowatt turbines. The project, which was erected in slightly deeper waters — 5 to 10 meters (sixteen to thirty-three feet) — than Vindeby, introduced a new foundation type, known as the "monopile," to the market. Unlike the steel tripods and concrete gravity-based foundations, the monopile is essentially a wide steel tube that is driven or drilled into the seafloor. The monopile is then capped by a transition piece, which supports the turbine's tower. The monopile would become the dominant foundation type for Europe's burgeoning offshore wind farm industry for the next twenty years.[16]

In 1995, Denmark installed its second offshore wind farm at Tunø Knob, similar in size to Vindeby with ten Vestas 500-kilowatt turbines erected on concrete gravity-based foundations in 3 to 5 meters (ten to sixteen feet) water depths. In 1996, the Netherlands built the biggest wind farm of the decade at Irene Vorrink. The project included the installation of twenty-eight Nordtank 600-kilowatt units for rated output of 16.8 megawatts.[17]

Sweden predicted in the early 1990s, based on the success of its single turbine installation at Nogersrund, that another ninety-seven turbines, grouped in seven wind farms, could be constructed along six miles of Baltic coast line. The government believed that sixty offshore wind farms could replace the country's twelve nuclear power plants.[18] However, Sweden would not construct its next first full-scale offshore wind farm until 1998. The project, erected in water depths ranging from 5.5 to 6 meters (eighteen to twenty feet) at Bockstigen, included five WindWorld 550-kilowatt turbines set this time on monopiles.[19]

The year 2000 marked the beginning of the use of multi-megawatt turbines for offshore wind farms and the migration toward deeper waters, the view being that the bigger the turbines in size, number, and output, the more economical offshore windpower would become. This technological shift would also help reduce the costs for offshore turbine foundations, installations, and power transmissions, which were nearly double that for landside turbines at the time.[20]

Britain commissioned its first offshore wind farm off Blyth Harbor in Northumberland. It included two Vestas 2-megawatt units installed on monopiles in 8.5 meters (twenty-eight feet) of water. At Utgrunden, Sweden, an offshore project of seven Enron Wind 1.4-megawatt turbines was installed in 6- to 10-meter (twenty to thirty-three feet) water depths. Denmark also broke an offshore wind industry record in 2000 by erecting twenty Bonus 2-megawatt turbines for a total rated power output of forty megawatts. The Netherlands' large Irene Vorrink wind farm had a rated capacity of only 16.8 megawatts. Europe, led by Denmark, the Netherlands, Sweden, and the United Kingdom, had now set the stage for the prospects of offshore windpower's further expansion and the rest of the world was starting to take notice of its abundant possibilities.[21]

In 2007, Post Denmark, in a postage stamp series, celebrated its 40-megawatt Middelgrunden offshore wind farm, built in 2000.

Chapter Four

Europe's Domination

By 2001, Europe's commitment to offshore wind energy development had started to accelerate, especially among those countries bordering the North and Baltic seas. In December that year, the European Wind Energy Association even convened a special conference on the topic of offshore wind energy, which attracted more than five hundred participants. The success of the earlier projects from the 1990s encouraged wind energy proponents and developers to take a closer look at the viability of generating electric power from ocean winds. Brian Braginton-Smith, a noted commenter and writer about offshore wind energy, described Europe's shift to offshore in geographic terms in a *Marine Technology Society Journal* article: "Limited undeveloped land area and wind resource constraints have led European nations to pursue wind energy offshore and this is seen as the next frontier in wind energy development."[1]

Europe's rich maritime legacy and North Sea oil and gas extraction capabilities enhanced its technical prowess and desire to erect wind turbines in the harshest waters. Other socio-economic factors have played significant roles in encouraging offshore wind energy development, including the European public's support for clean energy and government policies that help ensure economic sustainability of this fledgling industry.

Denmark

Just as it did in the mid-1970s to become an early leader in landside development of large wind turbines, Denmark quickly sailed to the forefront of offshore wind technology deployment at the turn of the twenty-first century. This occurred despite concerns that these projects could be abandoned in the wake of the Danish government's termination of a minimum price scheme for wind-based electric power in 1999. By 2002, Denmark built the world's largest offshore wind farm, Horns Rev, between 14 and 20 kilometers (nine to twelve miles) off its west coast in a rugged sea called Jutland. The wind farm consists of eighty Vestas 2-megawatt turbines for a total rated output of 160 megawatts. While Denmark celebrated Horns Rev's scale, the wind farm's image was slightly tarnished by technical setbacks in the winter of 2003 when the turbines'

transformers became afflicted by the salty ocean air. In the spring of 2004, it became apparent that the nacelles containing the generators had to be removed and replaced with hardier equipment. Even the blades were returned to the manufacturer for cleaning and to make minor repairs caused by lightning strikes and fatigue.[2]

Denmark did not allow this event to stop its offshore wind program. In 2003, the country witnessed the unveiling of three additional offshore wind farms. The island community of Samsø, as part of an attempt to generate 100 percent of its electricity from renewable energy sources, erected ten Bonus 2.3-megawatt turbines for a rated output of 23 megawatts. This was immediately followed by a 10.6-megawatt project consisting of four turbines at Frederikshaven. In the Baltic Sea, south of Nysted (Rødsand I), an offshore wind farm of seventy-two Bonus 2.3-megawatt machines with a total rated output of 158.4 megawatts was erected. Denmark continues to build ever-larger offshore wind farms, including the 2009 Horns Rev II, which includes ninety-one Siemens turbines for a total output of about 200 megawatts, and the 2010 Rødsand II with nearly the same number of Siemens turbines and comparable output. Together, the projects will generate enough power for 350,000 to 400,000 Danish homes.[3]

The Nysted offshore wind farm, completed in December 2003, includes seventy-two Bonus 2.3-megawatt turbines.
Courtesy of SEAS-NVE Holding A/S, Haslev, Denmark.

A panoramic aerial view of Denmark's 160-megawatt Horns Rev offshore wind farm.
Courtesy of Elsam A/S, Frederica, Denmark.

In September 2009, Denmark inaugurated the 209-megawatt Horns Rev II offshore wind farm in the Jutland Sea. *Courtesy of Dong Energy, Frederica, Denmark.*

While Denmark will be overtaken by larger offshore wind programs planned in other European countries, such as the United Kingdom and Germany, in the years ahead, the country's goal is to remain a world leader in terms of the highest amount of integrated wind-generated electricity consumed. "We need to remain a showcase for that so we can stay at the forefront on the technology side. Then Germany, the Netherlands or the United States will look at Denmark and see that's the way to do it," said Rune Birk Nielsen, spokesman for the Danish Wind Industry Association, in a February 2010 *New York Times* article.[4]

The Netherlands and Belgium

The Netherlands, steeped in windmill history and lore, has advocated modern windpower for the past thirty years. Most of its wind-generated electricity is produced on land, but a national effort has been underway since 2004 to take these developments to the coast when the government lifted a several-year-old ban on the construction of offshore wind farms in the North Sea. The ban required the adoption of new legislation before any new licenses for offshore wind farm projects would be issued.[5] In April 2007, the Dutch inaugurated the Egmond aan Zee offshore wind farm, which consists of thirty-six Vestas 3-megawatt turbines for a rated output of 108 megawatts, or enough electricity to power 100,000 Dutch households. The wind farm is managed by NoordzeeWind, a joint venture of Dutch utility Nuon and Royal Dutch Shell.[6]

In June 2008, Econcern and Eneco Energie started operations of the 120-megawatt Prinses Amalia wind park, located in the North Sea near Ijmuiden about 23 kilometers (fourteen miles) off the Dutch coast. The wind farm consists of sixty Vestas 2-megawatt turbines spread across fourteen square miles of sea surface, and produces enough power for about 125,000 Dutch homes.[7]

The Dutch government has set a goal to generate 6,000 megawatts of electricity from offshore windpower by 2020 and has identified sixty-five sites for this development in the North Sea and Ijsselmeer.[8] In February 2008, RWE of Germany submitted applications to the Dutch government to build two offshore wind farms with a final build-out of 2,000 megawatts. The first of the two projects, called Tromp Binnen, would start with fifty-nine turbines for an output of 300 megawatts and be located 75 kilometers (forty-six miles) offshore at Callantsoog.[9]

This unique image shows there is no doubt the front line of turbines puts the ones behind them in a strong wake.
Courtesy of Uni-Fly A/S, Esbjerg, Denmark.

Another lowland country, Belgium, has embarked on its own offshore wind projects. The Belgian government adopted legislation in 2002-2003 to receive and process applications for offshore wind farm development. The country's first project was erected in 2008-2009 about 30 kilometers (nineteen miles) off the coast from the port of Zeebrugge on the Thortonbank, a sandy shoal with a water depth of 20 to 30 meters (65 to 100 feet). In the first phase of the proposed 300-megawatt project, C-Power set up six of a planned sixty REpower 5-megawatt turbines on large gravity-based concrete foundations.[10]

Another developer, Belwind, began construction in late 2009 of a 330-megawatt offshore wind farm across 35 square kilometers (13.5 square miles) of the submerged Bligh Bank, which is about 50 kilometers (thirty-one miles) from Zeebrugge. By September 2010, Belwind had planned to complete the first phase of construction by having fifty-five turbines of 3 megawatts each in operation. The second and final phase of the wind farm will be completed in 2011.[11] Eldepasco was awarded a concession by the Belgian government to build a 144- to 216-megawatt wind farm on the Bank zonder Naam, about 38 kilometers (twenty-four miles) from the coast. The developer, which received its environmental permit in November 2009, plans to start construction in 2011.[12] The Belgian government has four additional concessions available to offshore wind farm developers with a total output of 2,000 megawatts.[13]

This aerial view shows the 330-megawatt Belwind offshore wind farm under construction in 2009 at Bligh Bank, about thirty miles from the Belgian port of Zeebrugge.
Courtesy of Belwind, Zeebrugge, Belgium.

Scandinavia and the Baltic

Early offshore wind leader Sweden continued work in this area, but at a much slower pace than Denmark. Since the installation of the 2.75-megawatt Bockstigen project in 1998 and the 10-megawatt Utgrunden facility in 2000, the country witnessed the construction of the 10-megawatt offshore wind farm at Yitre Stengrund in 2001. In the summer of 2008, Sweden's largest offshore wind farm, Lillgrund, was erected 10 kilometers (six miles) off the coast from Øresund near Malmö. The project, which is managed by Vittanfall AB, consists of forty-eight 2.3-megawatt Siemens turbines for a combined rated output of 110 megawatts or enough electricity for about 60,000 Swedish homes. The country inaugurated its first freshwater offshore wind farm in Vänern Lake near Gässlingegrund. The installation includes ten WinWinD 3-megawatt turbines located about 7 kilometers (four miles) from shore. Five of the ten turbines are owned by a local housing association and energy companies, with the rest owned by private companies, citizens, and economic associations.[14]

In 2009, three more large offshore wind farms were planned: Utgrunden II (90 megawatts), Vattenfall Karlskrona Vind (15 to 17.5 megawatts), and Kriegers Flak (640 to 1,000 megawatts). However, the projects have so far been postponed due to inconclusive "green certificates," and insufficient payment for offshore wind farm generated power. Thus Sweden's wind energy program has been focused onshore.[15] The Swedish Wind Energy Association estimates that the country will require an increase in wind energy production from the current two terawatt hours to about 20 terawatt hours, or about six to nine gigawatts, of which 2 to 3 gigawatts should come from offshore wind farms, in order for the country to make its binding 2020 renewable energy target.[16]

The Utgrunden offshore wind farm, built in 2000, is located at the Swedish Kalmar Sound between the mainland at Bergkvara and the Öland Island at Degerhamn. The operation includes seven General Electric 1.5-megawatt turbines. *Courtesy Vattenfall AB, Stockholm, Sweden.*

Other Scandinavian and Baltic countries have started exploring their offshore windpower potential. Norway approved its first offshore wind farm in September 2009. The first phase of the project, Havsul I, will be located off the coast of Møre and is planned to start generating 300 megawatts of power by 2011. However, as of mid-2010, the second phase, Havsul II, with a planned capacity of 800 megawatts, was still under consideration by the Norwegian government.[17]

Other Norwegian offshore wind farms planned are Siragrunnen south of Stavanger (200 megawatts) and Lista (1,000 megawatts).[18] In 2007, Finland erected a near-shore 13.8-megawatt wind farm at Åland Båtskär, followed in 2008 by the 30-megawatt Ajos wind farm at Kemi, which consists of ten turbines, two onshore and eight offshore. In 2007 and 2008, about 4,700 megawatts of offshore wind projects were identified. Off the country's west coast are the planned Pori I and Pori II projects at 36 and 30 megawatts respectively. In 2010, the Finnish government approved the 240-megawatt Kristiinankaupunki offshore wind farm, 10 kilometers (six miles) southwest of Närpö, which will help the country reach its goal of 500 megawatts of windpower by 2012.[19]

Two other large Finnish offshore wind farms are under consideration in the Bay of Bothania — Suurhieka, near Oulo, (400 megawatts), and Korsnäs (600 megawatts).[20] Poland, Estonia, Latvia, and Lithuania have all announced plans to investigate their offshore windpower potential as well. The Estonian government, for example, has received offshore wind park applications from Nelja Energia for a 700-megawatt offshore wind farm near Hiiumaa Island, Eesti Energija for a 700- to 1,000-megawatt project in Riga Gulf, and Neugrund to build a 190-megawatt wind farm in the Gulf of Finland along the northwestern coast of the country.[21]

This offshore wind farm of six turbines is located on the Nyhamn-Båtskär islands in the Åland archipelago southwest of Finland.
Photograph by Hannu Vallas of Finland.

United Kingdom and Ireland

One of today's most ambitious offshore wind energy programs may be found in the waters surrounding the United Kingdom. According to studies, the United Kingdom has the windpower generation potential for about 1,000 terawatt hours per year, or enough to meet the country's total electric consumption several times over.[22] The country has been often referred to in recent years as the "Saudi Arabia of offshore wind." However, the difference between measured windpower potential and actual offshore wind farm installation is vastly different, based on a myriad of issues such as economics, political and local support, availability of onshore grid connections, and geographic considerations. The United Kingdom has used a measured approach to its offshore wind energy program by approving increasingly larger projects in three separate rounds.

The first round initiated in December 2000 included a requirement for developers to lease offshore sites from the Crown Estate, the royal property manager. The Crown Estate, which dates to 1066, owns the seabed out to twelve nautical miles from the coast. Royalties paid for use of Crown Estate properties go to the treasury, which then supports the royals.[23] In April 2001, leases were awarded for eighteen projects at thirteen offshore locations. Since it was considered a pilot phase, Round 1 sites were limited to a maximum of thirty turbines. In December 2003, North Hoyle, with a capacity potential of sixty megawatts, became the first large-scale offshore wind farm to be installed under Round 1, followed by Scroby Sands (60 megawatts) in 2004, Kentish Flats (90 megawatts) in 2005, and Barrow (90 megawatts) in 2006.[24] One of the more interesting proposed offshore wind farms from Round 1 is the 150-megawatt Ormonde project, ten kilometers off Walney Island near Barrow, which, once built, will be the first large-scale offshore wind farm linked with another offshore energy source. In this case, Ormonde will combine wind energy with natural gas, so that when the wind is insufficient from the turbines, the power will come through conventional gas sources pumped from offshore fields in nearby Morecombe Bay. [25]

While the first round of projects was still underway, the British government in December 2003 approved a second round of fifteen projects with a combination of 7.2 gigawatts. While most of these projects were just starting construction in 2010, the individual outputs will be among some of the largest in the world, including Triton Knoll (1,200 megawatts), London Array (1,000 megawatts), Gwynt y Mor (750 megawatts), Race Bank (620 megawatts), and Docking Shoal and West Duddon, each at 500 megawatts. Most of these sites are located within the Thames Estuary, Greater Wash, and North West areas of the British coast.[26] The developers of the first phase of the London Array, 630 megawatts, expect to begin construction in 2011, followed by the completion of the second and final phases by 2014-2015.[27]

In January 2010, the government announced Round 3 of its offshore wind farm allocations, dwarfing all projects anywhere in the world thus far. The nine new offshore wind farm zones will offer a total combined output of 32 gigawatts, if fully developed, or provide enough power for every British home. The most massive proposed projects of Round 3 include Dogger Bank in the North Sea (9,000 megawatts), Norfolk Bank in the southern North Sea (7,200 megawatts), Irish Sea (4,100 megawatts), Hornsea in the North Sea (4,000 megawatts), and Firth of Forth off Scotland (3,400 megawatts).[28] Adam Bruce, chairman of the British Wind Energy Association, described the country's attitude toward offshore wind energy in a 2008 *Engineering & Technology* article:

> "We are at the forefront of an energy revolution that is about to transform the way in which we deliver electricity in this country – a revolution that will deliver energy to this generation, and the next, and the next, one that is indigenous and secure, and where the fuel is free."[29]

However, the country's need to embrace offshore wind energy is more about meeting its binding target within the European Union to generate at least twenty percent of its power from renewable energy sources by 2020.

Some of the thirty Vestas V90 turbines that make up the 90-megawatt Barrow offshore wind farm located in the East Irish Sea in the United Kingdom.
Courtesy of Barrow Offshore Wind Ltd., Berkshire, United Kingdom.

Neighboring Ireland has offshore wind energy aspirations of its own, but they currently are nowhere near the level and targets of the United Kingdom. Airtricity installed Ireland's first offshore wind turbines at Arklow Bank in 2004. The seven General Electric 3.6-megawatt turbines collectively produce about 25 megawatts. Arklow Bank is located on a sandbank about fifteen miles long and a half-mile wide off the coast of Arklow in County Wicklow.[30] The project is considered the first phase of what will ultimately be a 500-megawatt offshore wind farm. In 2008, the Irish government announced a new feed-in-tariff structure to encourage more offshore wind farm developments. The National Offshore Wind Association of Ireland, a group of five developers, expects the industry to collectively invest 4 billion euros ($4.9 billion) to develop nearly 5,000 megawatts of wind projects on existing lease areas off the Irish coast by 2020.[31] The Irish government has indicated that it may add another 3,000 megawatts worth of leases for offshore wind projects.[32]

European Wind Energy Association reported that Germany had collectively installed 25,777 megawatts of windpower, with all but two percent of that generated from landside turbines.[34] This occurred due to the country's lucrative 20-year feed-in tariffs for renewable energy sources. Although Germany forecasts that it could build another 10,000 megawatts of wind turbines onshore, the country has started to reach a level of maturity and more land is being excluded from large turbine construction.[35]

Offshore wind energy in Germany started gaining serious traction after the German parliament in June 2008 amended the Renewable Energy Act to raise the feed-in tariffs for offshore wind-generated power from nine cents to fifteen cents per kilowatt.[36] In late 2009, REpower Systems successfully completed installation of twelve 5-megawatt turbines at the offshore test field "alpha ventus," about 45 kilometers (twenty-eight miles) north of the island Borkum.[37]

Two of the seven General Electric 3.6-megawatt turbines at the 25.2-megawatt Arklow Bank wind farm off the coast of Ireland.

Germany

Closely rivaling offshore wind plans in the United Kingdom in the next twenty years will be Germany. Although a late starter in offshore wind energy compared to most of its neighbors, Germany has forty approved ocean sites in the North and Baltic seas with at least 20,000 megawatts of planned capacity.[33]

Germany is already by far the largest producer of wind-generated electricity in Europe. At the end of 2009, the

REpower Systems in late 2009 completed the installation of twelve 5-megawatt turbines at the offshore test field "alpha ventus" about twenty-eight miles north of the German island Borkum.
Courtesy of REpower Systems, Hamburg, Germany.

In October 2008, BARD Engineering GmbH inaugurated Germany's first 5-megawatt near-shore wind turbine prototype in 6.5- to 26-feet deep water at Hooksiel off the German North Sea coast. *Courtesy of BARD Gruppe, Emden, Germany.*

Supporting Infrastructure

The promise of larger offshore wind farms in Europe will require substantial investments to increase the efficiency and output of wind turbines, enhance capacity and capabilities of vessels used to transport and install the turbines, and further integrate the turbine supply chain in hub ports closest to the major offshore project areas. Europe is already fortunate to have longtime wind turbine manufacturers, like Siemens, Vestas, REpower, BARD, Multibrid, and Nordex, in its backyard. However, the need for turbine builders to have plants in individual European countries with offshore wind programs has increased since the early 2000s. Last year, a number of these companies, including several non-European players, such as General Electric, Mitsubishi Power Systems, and Clipper Windpower, announced plans to build wind turbine manufacturing plants in the United Kingdom. For example, Clipper's plant in Tyne, United Kingdom, will produce the 72-meter (236-foot) long blades for its Britannia Project, a 10-megawatt offshore wind turbine prototype that they plan to deploy off the British coast in late 2012.[38]

Clipper Windpower's 10-megawatt offshore wind turbine "Britannia" will be built at a plant in Tyne, United Kingdom. *Courtesy Clipper Windpower, Carpinteria, California.*

The biggest vessels in the European market currently handle up to four turbines of components per voyage, but to manage more intense construction schedules, vessels are under design with capacities for up to ten turbines worth of components and capabilities to operate in deeper waters (35 meters — or 115 feet — and beyond) and rougher seas in order to stretch the installation season to between 260 and 290 days.[39] Some designers envision vessels to accommodate completely quayside-built turbines, which will be placed intact on top of the foundations, minimizing most of the onboard crane activity that's associated with current offshore turbine installation practices. (See *Chapter 5* for more details.)

Some ports in Denmark and the Netherlands have developed specialties at handling offshore wind turbine components, but more of these facilities are needed to accommodate the expanding turbine component volumes of future projects. The British government has identified twenty-seven harbors with the potential of serving its offshore wind industry. However, ports to the east of England, in particular, still require substantial infrastructure investment to support this effort.[40] In recent years, Germany's Bremerhaven has pro-actively sought to become a hub port for the wind energy business. The promotional efforts of the Windenergie Agentur Bremerhaven/ Bremen, a wind industry network formed in 2002, have helped to attract more than a half dozen large turbine equipment suppliers and two research and development organizations to Bremerhaven in recent years.[41] Some Dutch developers have proposed creating a "harbor at sea" concept whereby man-made multipurpose platforms will serve as bases for offshore wind farm installations and maintenance operations.[42]

Specialized vessels, like this one used in 2009, were used to install the rotor and blades for a 5-megawatt turbine at Germany's "alpha ventus" test field. *Courtesy of REpower Systems, Hamburg, Germany.*

In late 2009, nine European Union members, including the United Kingdom, Germany, France, the Netherlands, Sweden, Denmark, Belgium, Ireland, and Luxembourg, agreed to a 565 million euro ($690 million) plan to develop a supergrid for offshore wind during the next two decades. Some connections between offshore wind farms are already underway, such as installation of cables linking projects in the Netherlands with Denmark, Norway with the United Kingdom, and Germany and the United Kingdom with the Netherlands. Christian Kjaer, chief executive officer of European Wind Energy Association, declared: "A European offshore grid would be good news for consumers as it would dramatically improve competition and move us a step further towards a real internal market in electricity."[44] To make the supergrid work, the association said HVDC (high voltage direct current) technology would be required because it offers "the controllability needed to allow the network both to transmit wind power and to provide the highway for electricity to trade, even between different synchronous zones. Moreover, HVDC offers the possibility of terminating inside onshore AC grids, and thus avoid onshore reinforcements close to the coast."[45]

In May 2010, components for the Siemens 3.6 MW turbines were unloaded at Harwich International Port in preparation for construction of the Greater Gabbard offshore wind farm, which will consist of 140 turbines and be able to provide a total of 504 megawatts of power. The Essex port has provided similar services for British offshore wind farms at Gunfleet Sands and Thanet Wind Farms earlier in 2010.
Courtesy of Harwich International Port, Essex, United Kingdom.

Supergrid

To more efficiently manage the flow of offshore wind-generated electric power to markets in the future, European governments and industry have embraced the concept of a sub-sea "supergrid" to connect offshore wind farms and link them to onshore power grids. The concept was first proposed in 2007 by Dr. Eddie O'Connor, former chief and founder of Ireland-based Airtricity and now head of Mainstream Renewable Power, to integrate the output from offshore wind farms along the United Kingdom, the Netherlands, and Germany.[43]

Eddie O'Connor, head of Mainstream Renewable Power, coined the term "supergrid" in 2007 to link Europe's offshore wind farms so that their electric output is more efficiently transferred to on-shore consumer markets.
Courtesy of Mainstream Renewable Power, Dublin, Ireland.

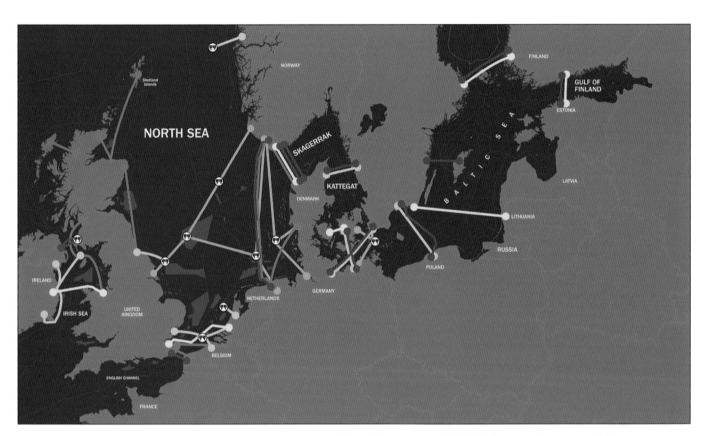

The offshore grid map for 2020 shows all the existing offshore transmission lines, all the planned lines, those currently under study, and the first ten years of the European Wind Energy Association's 20-Year Network Development Master Plan (gray lines), together with the concession zones. The association also makes its recommended offshore transmission lines through 2030 (see opposite page). *Courtesy of the European Wind Energy Association, Brussels, Belgium.*

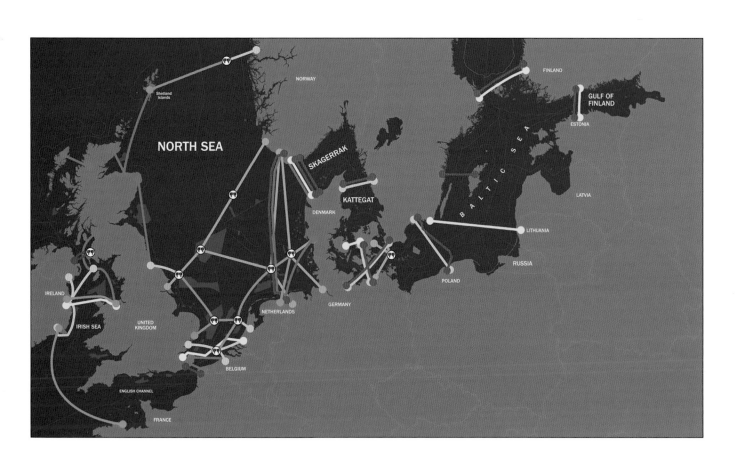

20-Year Outlook

In December 2008, the European Union members agreed to a binding target of generating twenty percent renewable energy within their individual borders by 2020, an ambitious undertaking that will require windpower to contribute at least twelve percent of the electricity collectively toward this goal. The European Wind Energy Association forecasts that the offshore wind industry will install up to 40 gigawatts of power by 2020, just under 1.5 gigawatts in 2010, which would produce 148 terawatt-hours of electricity, the equivalent of 3.6 to 4.3 percent of the European Union's electricity use depending on consumer demand. It's also expected that a quarter of Europe's total wind energy could be produced offshore by 2020.[46]

Furthermore, the association forecasts that by 2030 installed offshore wind capacity could reach 150 gigawatts, equal to between 12.8 and 16.7 percent of European Union electricity consumption, and that about half of all of Europe's windpower could be produced offshore by that time.[47] The association has confidence in its forecasts with more than 100 gigawatts of European offshore projects identified as either under construction, consented, or proposed by the end of 2010. "This 100 GW of offshore wind projects shows tremendous developer interest and provides a good indication that EWEA's expectation that 150 GW of offshore wind power will be operating by 2030 is both accurate and credible," the association said in its 2009 report *Oceans of Opportunity: Harnessing Europe's Largest Domestic Energy Resources*.[48]

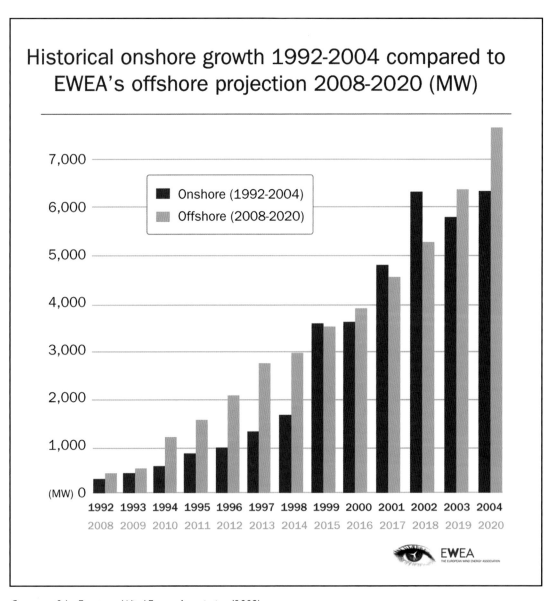

Courtesy of the European Wind Energy Association (2009), Brussels Belgium.

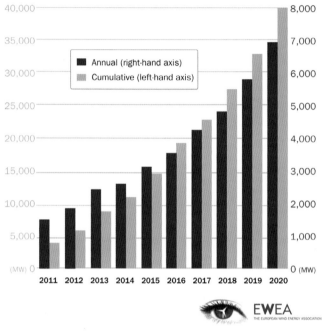

Courtesy of the European Wind Energy Association (2009), Brussels Belgium.

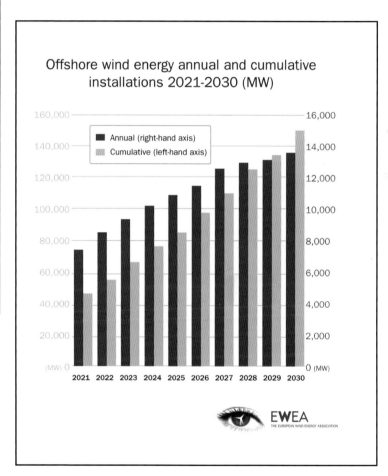

Courtesy of the European Wind Energy Association (2009), Brussels Belgium.

Chapter Five

Building Offshore Wind Farms

The installation of the first offshore wind turbines in the early 1990s was an unrefined activity involving the combination of landside wind energy specialists, marine engineers, and transportation and construction specialists from Europe's North Sea oil and gas sector. For the first ten years of the industry, these offshore wind farms were generally small, compared to today's projects, with turbines ranging in size from 450 to 600 kilowatts, and they were erected in relatively shallow coastal waters of 5 to 6 meters deep. The industry got by with the existing marine equipment for transporting and constructing these turbines.

Between 2000 and 2005, developers across Denmark, Sweden, and the United Kingdom began building bigger offshore wind farms with turbines in the range of 2 to 3 megawatts. By 2002, the giants among the projects included Denmark's Horns Rev with eighty Vestas 2-megawatt turbines and Nysted with seventy-two Bonus 2.3-megawatt machines. During this time, these wind turbines were also being erected in increasingly deeper water. Although smaller in size, Denmark's Samsø wind farm in 2003 included ten Bonus 2.3 megawatt turbines placed in a 20-meter (65-foot) water depth, and at the same time the North Hoyle, United Kingdom wind farm's thirty Vestas 2-megawatt machines were installed in water depths of 10 to 20 meters (33 to 65 feet). Also that year, an offshore wind farm at Arklow Bank, Ireland, which included seven GE Wind 3.6-megawatt turbines, reached a maximum depth of 25 meters (82 feet). These projects gave rise to specialist firms dedicated to the logistics management of offshore wind farm planning, construction, operations, and maintenance.

Site Analysis

Long before an offshore wind farm developer can start building, extensive research must be conducted of the perspective site, both above and below the water line. On the surface, average wind and weather conditions are thoroughly assessed to determine whether the site is conducive for operating the turbines. The prevailing winds that come off the water tend to be stronger than those that originate over the land.[1] Currently, the most common way to assess long-term wind conditions over coastal waters is by using meteorological towers and buoys. A new wind assessment technology, known as "mesoscale" modeling, is under development to better determine spatial and temporal distribution of offshore winds across a site.[2] Bruce Bailey, noted wind expert and president of AWS Truepower, said it's crucial to understand "the role the local sea breeze circulation plays in the offshore wind environment and its enhancement of windpower availability is an important factor in the site of offshore wind farms, especially within 30 km (nineteen miles) of the coast."[3] In U.S. waters, the most productive offshore winds are experienced during the warmer months.

Wave conditions must also be examined, including the potential impacts of major storms. Waves produce a variety of forces that can harm the long-term viability of offshore turbines.[4] Necessary underwater surveys are even more complex, requiring the use of a host of marine equipment capable of performing hydrographic and geophysical evaluations, high-resolution seismic work, and surveys of existing cables and other potential sub-sea hazards, such as shipwrecks and unexploded ordinance. Currents must be understood to prevent undue turbine foundation and cable erosion.[5]

Other studies must gauge shore-side public tolerance of offshore turbines dotting the coastal horizon, potential disruptions to vessel navigation and aircraft radar, and impacts on local and migratory bird populations. All of these studies must be reviewed and validated by regulatory authorities in charge of offshore marine resources and will likely be subject to routine public scrutiny. This arduous process may take years to accomplish, and despite the thoroughness and due-diligence exercised by a developer, the offshore wind farm may still be scuttled.

Attracting Investors

Back on land, the pre-planning stages for offshore wind farm developers are equally challenging. Developers must work through complex interactions with banks and investors to help finance the projects. While securing investor interest has become somewhat easier in recent years due to environmental awareness, renewable energy projects are still considered risky commercial investments, and they are closely weighed against the cost of power produced from traditional fossil fuel-based sources, such as coal, oil and natural gas. Whether to invest in wind power may come down to pennies on the dollar when all other costs, including capital, are factored into the equation. Offshore wind farm developers have found a more receptive investment community in Europe, based on the political support and strong government policies for wind energy and a general willingness among the public to accept paying a little extra for cleanly produced electricity. That type of momentum for offshore wind investment has only started in North America, and securing money for these projects remains a daunting task for developers.[6]

Other crucial pre-construction aspects that must be considered are finding utilities willing to purchase offshore-generated power and provide access to their grids. Without these agreements, an offshore wind farm would be rendered useless. Once these measures are in place, then the offshore wind farm developer can begin to firm its equipment and service provider contracts.

Setting Foundations

The process of offshore wind turbine installation begins with the sub-sea foundations. The type of foundation used by a developer depends on the water depth and installation requirements from the wind turbine manufacturer. Offshore wind turbine foundations trace their roots to the European offshore oil and gas industry, and have evolved over the past twenty years while wind farm developers have moved their projects into deeper waters.

The most commonly deployed foundation so far has been the monopile, essentially a large steel tube with a wall up to 60 millimeters (2.5 inches) thick and 6 meters (20 feet) in total diameter. Monopiles are generally used at water depths of less than 30 meters (100 feet). These structures are either transported on decks of vessels, or floated and pulled by towboat to location. Monopiles, which are also preferred for a sandy seabed, must be driven by large hydraulic hammers 20 to 30 meters (65 to 100 feet) below the mud line.[7] In 2009, 88 percent of Europe's installed wind farms used monopile foundations.[8]

NaiKun Wind Energy Group's meteorological tower measures weather conditions in the Hecate Strait off the coast of British Columbia. *Courtesy of NaiKun Wind Energy Group, Vancouver, British Columbia, Canada.*

Various types of offshore wind turbine foundations. *Courtesy of the National Renewable Energy Laboratory, Golden, Colorado.*

Another type of sub-sea structure used by some wind farm developers has been the gravity foundation. Although less frequently deployed, they are suitable in locations where shallow seabed rock is prevalent.[9] Gravity foundations are concrete structures prefabricated onshore, carried out by barge to the wind farm site and lowered into to the seabed. The largest deployment of gravity foundations took place during the construction of the Nysted wind farm at Rødsand, Denmark. The wind farm's seventy-two foundations weigh about 1,800 tons apiece in a water depth of 6 to 10 meters (20 to 33 feet).[10] To build in deeper waters, in the range of 30 to 60 meters (100 to 200 feet), developers are starting to use steel tripods or jacket foundations, which resemble steel truss structures, anchored to the ground by steel piles.[11] In June 2010, Vestas started a research program to construct jacket foundations for large turbines installed in water depths of up to 70 meters (230 feet).[12] A field of foundations, no matter what the type, is laid out in a uniform pattern, called an array, and the spacing between foundations is generally about 0.5 nautical miles.[13]

The jack-up vessel *Sea Jack* is preparing to monopile foundations at Denmark's Horns Rev 2 offshore wind farm in May 2000.
Courtesy of A2SEA, Fredericia, Denmark.

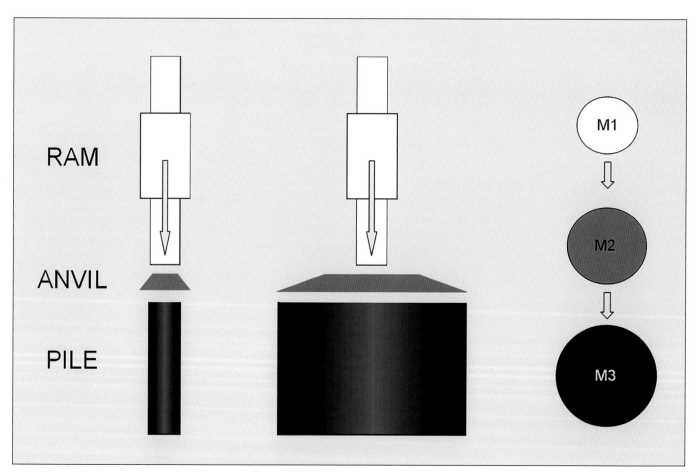

Main parts of the hydraulic hammer used to drive monopile foundations.
Courtesy of IHC Hydrohammer BV, Kinderdijk, the Netherlands.

A large hydraulic hammer was used to drive monopile foundations at the
Barrow offshore wind farm off the coast of the United Kingdom in 2006.
Courtesy of IHC Hydrohammer BV, Kinderdijk, the Netherlands.

Installing Turbines

Once the monopiles are set, the tops are fitted with transition pieces to ensure the foundations are level for the turbines that will be placed upon them. Each transition piece must be sealed with grout before construction of the topside turbines can actually begin. This process starts, often in cases involving large wind farms, while foundations are still being placed.[14]

Once the monopiles are in place, they are leveled with transition pieces before turbines are placed on them. These monopiles were installed for the offshore wind farm at Kentish Flats, United Kingdom in 2005. *Courtesy ep4 offshore, Winsen, Germany.*

Turbines are broken down into three main parts: the tower sections; nacelles, which contain the electrical power generating equipment; and the blades. Wind farm developers will try to amass the parts from their suppliers at a central seaport facility close to the offshore site. The turbine manufacturers will assemble as much of the units as possible onshore.[15] In some cases, this may include attaching two of the three blades to the rotor on the nacelle, described within the industry as "bunny ears." Specialized vessels retrieve the turbine components from the ports, often carrying enough on their decks for three to four complete units per trip to the offshore sites.

One of the unique features of the vessels is their "jack-up" legs, which come to rest on the seabed and raise the vessel hulls a couple of meters out of the water to provide stable platforms from which their cranes and crews can operate. On the water, these installation vessels are operated much like an assembly line, moving from one turbine site to the next and quickly returning to the port for more components.[16] This is no easy feat considering the ever-increasing size of the turbines used for offshore wind farms. In the early 1990s, the units produced less than a megawatt of power each. Now they produce an average of three to five megawatts, with plans underway for turbines that will produce from 6 to 10 megawatts of power.

The European Wind Energy Association reported in 2009: "This trend is motivated by the quest for economies of scale, although the nacelle weight puts constraints on the installation vessels."[17] Subsequently, the physical size of the turbines has also grown, with rotor diameters now reaching 80 to 126 meters (263 to 413 feet), but, unlike their landside counterparts, offshore units use shorter towers because the wind shear profiles on the sea are more gradual.[18]

The jack-up vessel *Sea Power* installs a turbine tower at Sweden's Lillgrund offshore wind farm in 2007. *Courtesy of A2SEA, Fredericia, Denmark.*

Complete wind turbine rotor and blade sets are loaded on-board the jack-up vessel *Sea Power* for delivery to the Lillgrund offshore wind farm in 2007. *Courtesy of A2SEA, Fredericia, Denmark.*

A wind turbine blade is lifted from the deck of the jack-up vessel *Resolution* for attachment to the rotor.
Courtesy of MPI Offshore, North Yorkshire, United Kingdom.

A large crane raises blades for the offshore wind turbines at Horns Rev in June 2002.
Courtesy of A2SEA, Fredericia, Denmark.

Wind turbine installations depend on the season when the sea is less prone to major storms. Sixty to seventy percent of the turbine installation work in Europe, for instance, is done in the summer. When the weather cooperates, one turbine can be erected about every thirty-six hours. Work must stop when the winds reach 12 to 15 meters per second (about 25 to 32 mph) or the waves exceed 2 to 2.5 meters (6.5 to 8 feet).[19]

The efficiency of turbine installation ships have continued to improve. In 2000, naval architect Kurt Thomsen foresaw a niche in designing wind industry-specific vessels instead of relying on equipment from the offshore oil and gas sector. His early efforts in this area led to the conversion of two former containerships to self-elevating platform vessels in 2001 and 2002 respectively, and thus establishing Danish company A2SEA. Placed on the deck of each A2SEA vessel was a 450-ton crane with 110 tons of lift, capable of raising turbine components 80 meters (about 263 feet) high and 20 to 22 meters (about 65 to 72 feet) away from the side of the ship.[20] A2SEA's vessels are operated by a crew of thirteen, with additional technical experts from the turbine manufacturers and wind farm developers raising the number of people on board to near thirty.[21] Shortly after A2SEA's market success, Marine Projects International in the United Kingdom became the first company to introduce a purpose-built wind turbine installation vessel to the market. In addition to cranes for setting up the turbines, the vessel, named the *Resolution*, included a 160-ton onboard hydraulic hammer and cable-laying equipment.[22]

In 2010, there were about ten vessels dedicated to offshore wind turbine installation work in the North and Baltic seas. The race is on to increase the size of the turbine installation vessel fleet. It's estimated that twenty vessels will be in place by 2013-2014, followed by twenty-five vessels by 2015-2016 and thirty vessels by 2017-2020.[23] This will still not be enough vessel capacity to satisfy all the needs of the numerous offshore wind projects planned not just for Europe, but also in North America and Asia in the next decade. In February 2010, the Community of European Shipyards' Association and the European Wind Energy Association called on the European Commission and the European Investment Bank to support the building of new ships to serve the expanding offshore wind energy market in the coming years. Investments in new ships totaling 2.4 billion euros ($2.9 billion) will be needed for the predicted growth of offshore wind.[24]

The *Resolution*, with legs firmly placed against the seabed, while in port awaiting a load of wind turbine components.
Courtesy of MPI Offshore, North Yorkshire, United Kingdom.

How the legs of a jack-up vessel appear underwater.
Courtesy of A2SEA, Fredericia, Denmark.

The newest installation vessels will be larger than their predecessors in order to handle the bigger turbines coming on line and to jack up in deeper waters. Clipper Windpower has started work on a 10-megawatt turbine called the Britannia and Denmark's Risø National Laboratory has a 20-megawatt model with 250-meter (320-foot) diameter blades on the drawing board. In response to these turbine trends, Bard Group in June 2009 launched the Wind Lift I. This vessel can work in maximum water depths of 45 meters (148 feet) and has an onboard crane capable of lifting and installing the company's 5-megawatt wind turbines.[25]

Master Marine AS of Norway is building jack-up installation barges that will work at water depths of 98 meters (322 feet) with two onboard cranes capable of lifting 750 tons each and room for up to 260 people.[26] Similarly, HochTief Construction AG and Beluga Shipping GmbH in Germany plan to build two of four offshore wind farm installation vessels by 2012, with platforms measuring 135 x 40 meters (443 x 131 feet), 600-ton lift cranes and carrying capacities for 8,000 tons and up to two hundred people. The jack-up legs of these vessels will allow the companies to work in water depths of up to fifty meters (164 feet). The companies claim each vessel will efficiently handle about eighty turbines a year.[27] However, none of these purpose-built vessels are cheap. Depending on the equipment requirements, they could cost in the range of $150 to $350 million each.[28]

The Wind Lift I at the outer Ems estuary on course to Emden, Germany, after departing the Lithuanian shipyard at Klaipeda in mid-2009 on its maiden voyage. *Courtesy of BARD Gruppe, Emden, Germany.*

The jack-up vessel Wind Lift I during a 2009 test in the Baltic Sea. The vessel is designed to sit in water with depths of nearly one hundred feet. *Courtesy of BARD Gruppe, Emden, Germany.*

Installation vessels are also expected to further evolve as wind farm developers and turbine manufacturers seek ways to lessen sea-based construction steps. The cost to install a turbine at sea, in 2010, was estimated at about 4 million euros ($4.9 million) per megawatt of capacity, compared to about 1.5 million euros ($1.8 million) per megawatt on land.[29] Keppel AmFELS's proposed KATI installation vehicle, a joint design with Glaston Associates, will be capable of transporting up to three pre-constructed 6-megawatt turbines to offshore sites where they will essentially be lowered onto pre-set monopiles or other deeper water platforms, eliminating the need for a costly onboard crane. In 2009, a typical onboard crane cost more than $45 million.[30] The payloads could become much larger over time with some designers aiming for vessels capable of carrying enough components for ten to twelve turbines at a time.

An artist rendering of Keppel AmFELS's KATI installation vehicle, a joint design with Glosten Associates, is capable of transporting up to three pre-constructed 6-megawatt turbines to offshore sites where they are lowered onto preset monopiles without use of an onboard crane.
Courtesy of Keppel AmFELS Ltd., Singapore.

Laying Cable

The "lifeline" of any offshore wind farm is the network of cables that carry electricity generated by the individual turbines to the shore. Starting inside the turbine itself may be several kilometers of wiring connecting the various power generating equipment and systems monitoring electronics.[31] The voltage output of each turbine is about 33 kilovolts.

The companies that perform the offshore wind farm cabling come from the marine telecom and oil and gas industries. "We apply what we've learned from our telecom experience to offshore wind farms, meaning we have been able to exploit our many years of expertise in areas such as route planning, vessel scheduling and vessel selection. In many cases, we are also able to use our fleet of vessels, sub-sea plows and remotely operated vehicles (ROVs) for cable installation and post-installation burial and inspection in the offshore wind sector," said Ian Gaitch, sales director of Global Marine Systems, Energy, one of the largest cable laying operators in the world.[32]

The Atlas 1 is a powerful, state of the art cable working ROV (remotely operated vehicle), designed for cable maintenance, post lay, and inspection roles. With 300 kilowatts of installed power, Atlas 1 has substantial cable intervention and burial capability and a range down to about a mile of water depth.
Courtesy of Global Marine Systems, Energy, Essex, United Kingdom.

The Atlas I ROV with TSS cable tracking frame deployed. *Courtesy of Global Marine Systems, Energy, Essex, United Kingdom.*

The cable laying process generally starts with the installation of the cable end into the "J-tube" fixed to the foundation of each turbine. A vessel will then install the cable towards the next turbine foundation and perform the same activity. The process continues as per the offshore wind farm design until all the turbines are connected in rows or strings linked to a central offshore substation, which converts the 33 kilovolts from each turbine to 132 kilovolts to prevent any grid loss as the power is transmitted by the export cable to the shore-side power grid.[33]

This offshore transformer substation is for the Nysted offshore wind farm at Rødsand, Denmark. The 72 Bonus 2.3-megawatt turbines in the farm transmit electricity to the substation via underwater cables, which in turn transmit the electric power to the onshore power grid.
Courtesy of Nysted Havmøllerpark, Gedser, Denmark.

Plough being deployed with cable entering plough bellmouth.
Courtesy of Global Marine Systems, Energy, Essex, United Kingdom.

There are many factors to consider when laying cable from the offshore wind farm to the shore. Issues like water depth at the shore landing, cable congestion at the offshore transformer platform and prevailing weather conditions all need to be evaluated. Export cables are large and heavy. Some of the latest cables under production are 220 millimeters (nine inches) in diameter and weigh 90 tons per kilometer. In order to load and lay these cables efficiently, a vessel must have a large turntable or carousel. Cable installation contractors must also have a clear understanding of the seabed geography along the cable routes.[34]

Like the installation vessel operators, cable layers are under pressure to further develop their equipment and efficiency to meet increasing demand. Global Marine Systems is designing new vessels for future large wind farms that will be much further out to sea. These vessels will have a large lift capacity of up to 7,000 tons on a turntable and will have the power to simultaneously plow in the cables without the need for using an anchor spread.[35]

Operations and Maintenance

Once an offshore wind farm is operational, it requires continuous monitoring and maintenance. Due to location and potential for inhospitable weather, this type of wind farm is difficult to service. Simon-Philippe Breton and Geir Moe wrote in a 2009 *Renewable Energy* article about the heavy costs and logistics challenges associated with providing timely maintenance to offshore wind farms:

> "Repairs are an estimated 5-10 times more expensive to perform offshore than onshore, mainly due to the need for expensive crane vessels, and waiting periods for suitable weather conditions can be extremely costly. In some cases, even for a turbine located only 1 km (or about a half mile) offshore, a period as long as two weeks can pass without access to the site for repair being possible."[36]

Turbine manufacturers have learned a number of costly lessons associated with offshore wind farms in the North and Baltic seas. In 2005, Vestas had to remove and repair eighty turbine generators from Denmark's Horns Rev 1 wind farm after two years of operation due to the corrosive effects of salt-laden ocean air.[37] The need for significant repairs have also been experienced below the water line. In August 2008, the 4-megawatt Blyth offshore wind farm in the United Kingdom, commissioned in 2000, spent nearly six months offline while the operator replaced the export cable with a specially armored cable imported from Italy.[38]

While most maintenance issues involving offshore wind farms are less dramatic, seawater remains the biggest enemy of these structures. The most vulnerable area of the turbines is the "splash zones," where most of the waves will hit with a combination of saltwater and high oxygen content. If the outside surface of the turbine structure is not sufficiently protected by special offshore epoxy based coatings, corrosion will occur. Within two to three years of operation, some turbines in the United Kingdom's North Hoyle and Ireland's Arklow Banks wind farms have experienced serious corrosion at their base supports due to inadequate protective coatings.[39] Lightning strikes on turbine blades are more prevalent offshore and may pose significant logistical difficulties in making repairs.

A direct cable shore-end landing.
Courtesy of Global Marine Systems, Energy, Essex, United Kingdom.

Through early 2010, no offshore wind farms maintained full-time technicians on-site, although many new substations now offer small equipment storage and survival rooms for technicians stranded due to sudden changes in weather.[40] The work in general poses numerous safety challenges for technicians. While helicopters have been used to lower personnel to nacelles on the top of the turbine towers, this is often cost prohibitive as well as a significant risk to helicopter crews. Vessels are the most common form of technician transport. Reaching the ladder at the base of a turbine from a bobbing vessel takes a great deal of timing, skill and confidence on the part of the technician. Then, once inside the tower, the technician must make the 80 to 100 meter (263 to 328 feet) climb to the nacelle. It is unclear how many injuries or deaths have resulted from offshore wind turbine construction and maintenance during the past twenty years, since the industry does not maintain a related index.[41]

Delivering technicians by helicopter to the top of REpower's offshore wind turbines.
Courtesy of Wiking Helikopter Service GmbH, Sande, Germany.

Turbine manufacturers are starting to develop machines specific to the ocean environment, rather than the traditional practice of transferring onshore turbines offshore. Offshore units will require improved condition-monitoring systems, automatic bearing lubrication systems, onboard service cranes, and oil temperature regulations systems, all at levels that exceed the performance for on-shore turbines.[42] REpower claims its new 5-megawatt turbines are robust enough to be serviced only once a year.[43] Yet, technicians will continue to interact with turbines, and to improve the safety associated with the "leap" between maintenance vessel and turbine, some engineering firms have designed safer, more stable personnel transfer mechanisms.

In 2007, a group of Dutch engineers from Delft University developed a device for the decks of maintenance vessels, dubbed the Ampelmann, which employs a system of hydraulic legs, similar to a flight simulator, that sense vessel movements on the water and offer a stable platform on which technicians can cross over to the turbine.[44] Another example of improved technician safety devices is German engineer Heinrich Duden's Personal Transfer System (PTS), which uses a crane to lift a technician from the maintenance vessel to the turbine. The crane's winch counterbalances the vertical movement of the vessel.[45]

A personal transfer system, known as PTS, during testing in Hamburg, Germany. German engineer Heinrich Duden, designer of the PTS, is in an immersion suit life-vest, harness, and some of the PTS equipment. *Courtesy ep4 offshore, Winsen, Germany.*

An artist rendering of the vessel model *Wind Express 28*, one of Austral's new range of high-speed transfer vessels specifically designed for the burgeoning offshore wind farm industry.
Courtesy of Austral, Henderson, Australia.

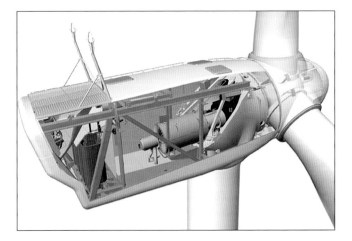

A cut-away diagram showing the nacelle interior of one of the thirty-six Vestas V90-3.0 turbines at the Egmond aan Zee offshore wind farm in the Netherlands. The large electrical transformers are in red, the generator is colored light blue and the gear box/transmission is dark green. *Courtesy NoordzeeWind, Ijmuiden, the Netherlands.*

Operations and maintenance will be further challenged to keep up with ever-changing turbine technologies. For example, to reduce the number of moving parts in the nacelles and hopefully the level of maintenance, some turbine manufacturers are developing gearless or direct-drive wind turbines. Siemens' direct-drive 3-megawatt machine has lower height and weight than its 2.3-megawatt machine and half the number of moving parts. In the traditional wind turbine, a gearbox and rotor are connected to a generator to start the flow of current, while the Siemens direct-drive machine has a permanent magnet attached to the rotor, which connects directly to a generator, eliminating the need for the gearbox.[46] General Electric also entered the direct-drive offshore wind generator business in 2010 after it acquired ScanWind of Sweden the year before.[47]

A technician accesses the base of a wind turbine tower at the Burbo Bank offshore wind farm. Owned by Dong Energy of Denmark, the 25-turbine, 90-megawatt operation is located on the Burbo Flats in Liverpool Bay at the entrance of the River Mersey in the United Kingdom.
Courtesy of Wind Power Works, Global Wind Energy Council, Brussels, Belgium.

In 2007, Dutch engineers developed a device, dubbed the Ampelmann, to transfer technicians from a maintenance vessel to the offshore wind turbine tower base using a system of hydraulic legs for stabilization.
Courtesy of Ampelmann Operations BV, Delft, the Netherlands.

Typical Building Process For An Offshore Wind Farm

The building process for a typical offshore wind farm.
Courtesy of REpower Systems, Hamburg, Germany; illustration by Keith Higginbotham, Long Beach, California.

Chapter Six

North American Takeoff

The United States effectively entered offshore wind farm development with the April 28, 2010 Department of the Interior's approval to begin construction of a large wind farm off the Massachusetts coast at Cape Cod. The approval was anything but easy for Cape Wind Associates, the developer of the Cape Cod wind farm, to obtain. For nine years, the project plodded along, routinely delayed by a federal bureaucracy unsure how to regulate offshore wind energy, numerous environmental impact studies, and a politically charged opposition on Cape Cod.

Cape Wind traces its roots to 2000 when the principals of Massachusetts-based Energy Management Inc., led by Founder and President Jim Gordon, studied the migration toward offshore wind farms in Northern Europe, and believed the United States should do the same with its abundant coastal wind resources. In 2001, Cape Wind Associates, a subsidiary of EMI, announced its intention to construct a 130-turbine offshore wind farm, five miles off the coast of Cape Cod and covering a 25-square-mile area of the Nantucket Sound, called Horseshoe Shoal because of its shape. Cape Wind picked the site for its strong winds, shallow water, minimal storm wave heights, and proximity to an efficient landside electric transmission system.[1] With the potential to generate about 450 megawatts of power, the wind farm could effectively meet three-quarters of the electric power needs on Cape Cod and the surrounding islands, or about 400,000 homes. The positive environmental impact included replacing coal-fired power plants with a clean energy source.

In 2001, Jim Gordon, founder and president of Energy Management Inc., proposed to build a 450-megawatt offshore wind farm five miles off the coast of Cape Cod, Massachusetts. *Courtesy of Cape Wind Associates, Boston, Massachusetts.*

Cape Wind financed and supported several years of detailed environmental studies of offshore wind turbine impacts on local and migratory birds and mammals, commercial and military aviation, and fishing and vessel navigation. In November 2004, the Army Corps of Engineers issued a favorable 3,800-page Draft Environmental Statement that examined every aspect of the Cape Wind project.[2]

When the Bush administration signed the Energy Policy Act into law in 2005, Cape Wind spent the next three years essentially repeating the federal approval process under the Department of the Interior's Mineral Management Service, which took over offshore wind energy oversight from the Corps of Engineers. For more than forty years, the Mineral Management Service has governed the U.S. offshore oil, gas, and mineral extraction industries in federal waters, known as the Outer Continental Shelf. Federally controlled waters generally cover three miles off the coast out to 200 miles. Numerous state agencies are also involved in near-shore activities associated with offshore wind farms, including environmental protections and underwater cabling, all of which impact the approval process and construction timeframes. In May 2005, the Massachusetts Energy Facilities Siting Board approved Cape Wind's electric interconnection application. The state completed its final environmental assessment of the project in March 2007, favoring Cape Wind to move forward. The Mineral Management Service's Environmental Impact Statement was issued in January 2008, essentially repeating

the findings of the Corps of Engineer's report.[3] Press reports in late 2007 estimated Cape Wind by that time spent close to $25 million meeting both federal and state regulatory requirements for the project.

Yet Cape Wind was not a done deal and continued to face strong opposition led by local politicians and wealthy beachfront landowners under the Alliance to Protect Nantucket Sound. Others joined the opposition including fishermen and ferryboat operators, citing interruptions and risks to their livelihood. In their book, *Cape Wind: Money, Celebrity, Class, Politics and the Battle for Our Energy Future*, authors Wendy Williams and Robert Whitcomb provided insightful details into the nasty war of words that erupted between supporters and opponents of the Cape Wind project. The opposition noted that it was not opposed to windpower in general, but believed the sight of Cape Wind's offshore turbines would damage the historical and environmental attributes of Nantucket Sound. Cape Wind's Gordon endured attacks against his character over the years, but many believe his personal conviction toward offshore wind energy as a viable renewable energy source to reduce greenhouse gas emissions and the country's need to cut back dependence on imported oil saw him through. He also firmly believed in the consumer benefits associated with the project's wind-generated power. A study conducted on behalf of Cape Wind by Charles River Associates found that the wind farm should reduce wholesale electric prices in New England by $4.6 billion over twenty-five years, resulting in an average savings of $185 million per year.[4]

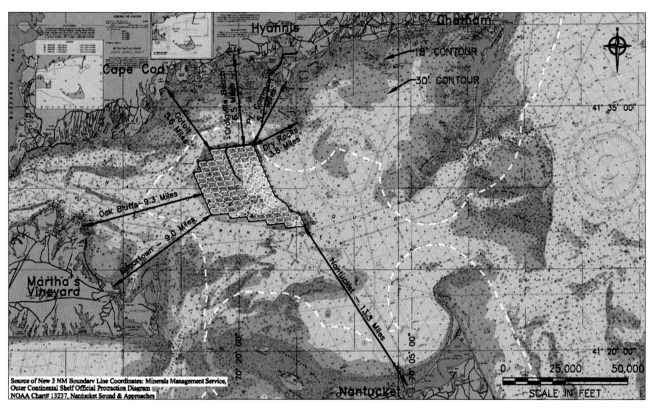

Map showing parameters of the Cape Wind offshore wind farm.
Courtesy of Cape Wind Associates, Boston, Massachusetts.

In early 2010, Cape Wind was almost derailed when the Mashpee Wampanoag tribe of Cape Cod and the Aquinnah Wampanoag on Martha's Vineyard requested that Nantucket Sound be placed on the National Register of Historic Places. The tribes argued that the wind farm would disturb their sunrise ritual and submerged Indian burial grounds.[5] There was also concern whether President Obama, who the late Sen. Edward Kennedy, a noted opponent of Cape Wind, endorsed for president, would ultimately support Cape Wind's go-ahead.[6] If Cape Wind failed to be approved, other proposed offshore wind projects throughout the country risked a similar fate, warned wind industry proponents.

"After careful consideration of all the concerns expressed during the lengthy review and consultation process and thorough analyses of the many factors involved, I find that the public benefits weigh in favor of approving the Cape Wind project at the Horseshoe Shoal location," said U.S. Interior Secretary Ken Salazar from the Boston State House on April 28, 2010. "With this decision we are beginning a new direction in our nation's energy future, ushering in America's first offshore wind energy facility and opening a new chapter in the history of this region." He attempted to assure opponents of Cape Wind that the Obama administration would closely oversee the wind farm's construction. "Impacts to the historic properties can and will be minimized and mitigated and we will ensure that cultural resources will not be harmed or destroyed during the construction, maintenance, and decommissioning of the project," Salazar said.[7]

"What enabled Cape Wind to reach this crucial milestone is the steadfast support of leading environmental, labor, health and trade organizations and the support of the overwhelming majority of Massachusetts citizens who have repeatedly made their voices heard. We also appreciate Governor Deval Patrick's support, vision and leadership to make Massachusetts a global leader in offshore renewable and the clean energy economy. Thank you to all those who made this day possible," Gordon said in a statement released the same day as the Interior Department's announcement.[8] The Alliance to Protect Nantucket Sound responded by filing lawsuits to continue their attempt to delay Cape Wind's rollout.[9]

Despite the lingering opposition, Cape Wind had planned to start constructing its offshore wind farm before the end of last year. A month prior to the Department of the Interior's approval, Cape Wind entered an agreement with Siemens to supply 130 3.6-megawatt turbines. The Siemens 3.6-megawatt machines are considered an industry "workhorse" with 1,000 units sold and 150 installed and successfully operating.[10] On May 7, 2010, New England utility National Grid entered a fifteen-year power purchase contract with Cape Wind to buy fifty percent of the wind farm's output starting in 2013. National Grid, which is obligated by Massachusetts' Green Communities Act to enter into long-term contracts to purchase at least three percent of its electricity supply from renewable generators,

said the cost to buy the power from Cape Wind will add $1.59 to each customer's monthly bill.[11]

The U.S. Department of Energy's National Renewable Energy Laboratory (NREL), based in Boulder, Colorado, has conducted numerous studies during the past decade into the potential electric power generation from U.S. offshore winds. The U.S. coastline, including Great Lakes shores, measures about 35,000 miles and the Offshore Continental Shelf covers about 1.7 billion acres of submerged land. According to NREL, about 430 gigawatts of wind capacity are accessible in coastal water depths of zero to 30 meters (100 feet), increasing to 970 gigawatts at water depths of up to 60 meters (200 feet). When including the country's deepwater potential, or water depths up to 900 meters (about a half mile), the total U.S. offshore wind resources comes to more than 2,500 gigawatts.[12] Twenty-eight of the contiguous forty-eight states with coastal boundaries use seventy-eight percent of the country's electricity, or about 2,769 terawatt-hours of the 3,548 terawatt-hours consumed nationwide in 2004. NREL has found that twenty-six of the twenty-eight coastal states have sufficient wind resources to meet at least twenty percent of their electricity requirement, and some states could even supply 100 percent of their electricity with full exploitation of their offshore wind resources.[13]

Massachusetts has been on the forefront of coastal states with an interest in developing its offshore wind resources. In January 2010, the state released the nation's first comprehensive plan to protect marine resources and develop sustainable uses of the state's ocean waters. The plan sets standards for the development of community and commercial scale offshore wind energy, and creates a formal role for regional planning authorities in wind energy. In specific, the plan covers the management of coastal waters from 0.3 nautical miles to the three-mile limit of state control. In two areas comprising just two percent of the planning area, the plan identifies zones suitable for commercial-scale wind energy development. These sites are located at Cuttyhunk Island and Normans Land, an uninhabited island about three miles southwest of Martha's Vineyard.[14] According to a *Boston Globe* article, the offshore commercial zone could support 166 turbines capable of powering up to 200,000 homes. This output could be expanded much further if turbines are approved for adjacent federal waters.[15]

Offshore community-scale wind projects for Massachusetts have been a difficult sale to small municipalities due to cost concerns. Since 2008, the town of Hull, located 13 kilometers (eight miles) east-southeast of Boston in the southern end of the Boston Harbor entrance, has considered erecting four 3-megawatt turbines offshore. The town is located at what's historically known as Windmill Point and has been a proponent of wind energy since the 1980s. In December 2001, Hull erected a Vestas 660-kilowatt turbine to replace a smaller aging unit, and added another 1.8-kilowatt turbine from Vestas in 2006. The output from these two turbines supplies eleven percent of Hull's annual electricity.[16] Although the addition of the four offshore wind turbines would have been enough to meet Hull's entire electric power requirement, last year the town government set aside the project over concerns electricity rates would rise by twenty-five percent.[17]

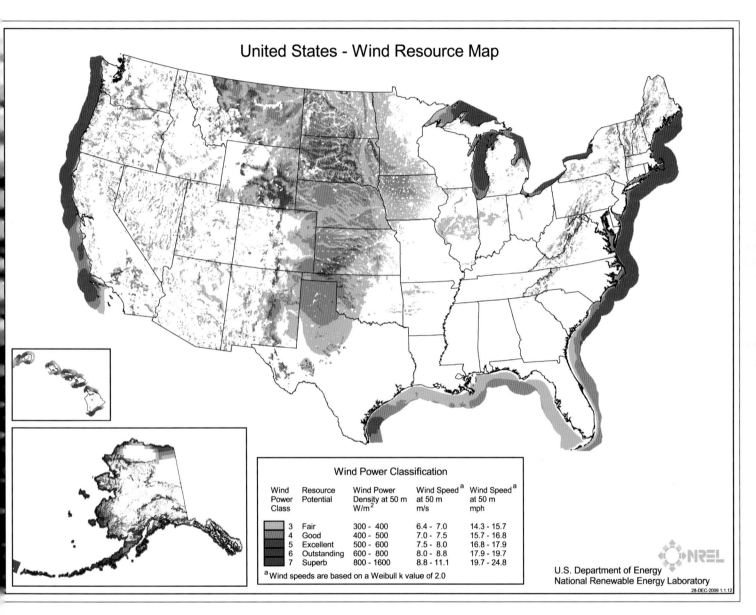

Twenty-six U.S. coastal states have sufficient winds to meet at least twenty percent of their electricity requirement, and some states could even supply 100 percent of their electricity with full exploitation of their offshore wind resources. *Courtesy of the National Renewable Energy Laboratory, Golden, Colorado.*

New England

Massachusetts' neighbor Rhode Island, led by Governor Donald L. Carcieri, is another New England state aggressively seeking to use its offshore winds to generate electric power. In 2008, the state appointed Deepwater Wind to develop a $1.2 billion offshore wind farm that will provide 1.3 million megawatt hours per year, or fifteen percent of all the electricity used in the state.[18] The 385-megawatt project will consist of 107 3.6-megawatt turbines located about seventeen miles off the Rhode Island coast. Deepwater, as the company's name implies, plans to use a 300-ton jacket of up to 160-foot length upon which to erect wind turbines in deeper waters. To support the construction of this offshore wind farm, in June 2009 Rhode Island enacted a law requiring National Grid, the state's main utility, to negotiate long-term contracts with renewable energy providers. These power purchase agreements are critical for developers to secure financing.[19]

However, Rhode Island and Deepwater suffered a setback in April 2010, when a twenty-year power purchase agreement reached by Deepwater and National Grid for a small five-to-eight turbine offshore wind farm within three miles off the coast of Block Island was rejected by the Public Utilities Commission stating that the market cost for Narragansett Electric ratepayers would be half a billion dollars higher over the life of the proposed contract.[20] The plan was for the Block Island wind farm to be operational by 2012, and help replace the island's dependence on five maintenance-prone CAT diesel generators.[21] For Deepwater, Block Island was supposed to be a demonstration project to attract additional financing for other potential offshore wind projects in the region.

In addition to Rhode Island, Deepwater, with PSEG Renewables, formed Garden State Offshore Energy to develop offshore wind projects serving New Jersey. In October 2008, the New Jersey Board of Public Utilities picked Garden States Offshore Energy to build a 350-megawatt offshore wind farm, which calls for ninety-six turbines arranged in a rectangular array sixteen to twenty miles off the coast of Cape May and Atlantic counties. The state plans for the entire project to be operational by 2013. The New Jersey Energy Master Plan calls for twenty percent of the state's energy, or 3,000 megawatts, to be generated by renewable energy sources by 2020. The state plans to meet most of this power quota through offshore wind energy.[22]

There are also three other offshore wind projects under study off New Jersey, including two in federal waters and one in state waters.

Perhaps one of the more interesting wind farm developments planned off the coast of New Jersey will be developed by Fishermen's Energy. While many commercial fishermen balked at the prospect of erecting wind turbines in coastal fishing grounds, a group of Northeast fishermen in the spring of 2007 decided to embrace it. The fishermen also believe they understand the sea from the surface to the seafloor better than anyone. Offshore wind farms also offer the fishing industry's workers job opportunities in construction, operations, and maintenance.[23] Fishermen's Energy developed a plan for constructing two wind farms off the coast of New Jersey, starting with an eight-turbine 20-megawatt project in state waters by 2012 and followed by a 66-turbine 350-megawatt development ten miles off the coast by 2014. In late April 2010, Fishermen's Energy set up a buoy 2.8 miles off the coast of Atlantic City, New Jersey, equipped with scientific instruments, to measure both wind and whale activity over the next two years.[24]

New York has considered the development of offshore wind farms along its Atlantic Coast waters since 2005. A controversial offshore wind farm was proposed along the southern coast of Long Island. The Long Island Power Authority (LIPA) wanted to erect forty turbines capable of generating 140 megawatts, but abandoned the project in August 2007, citing high costs as the reason.[25]

However, the power authority has not abandoned the offshore wind farm concept, and in April 2009, together with Consolidated Edison, formed a wind collaborative to advance the LIPA-ConEdison Offshore Wind Farm project. The project would be sited about thirteen miles off the Rockaway Peninsula and would likely be designed for 350 megawatts with the ability to expand to 700 megawatts. If approved, the first phase of the wind farm could come on line by 2015.[26]

Maine wants offshore wind to become a key ingredient in its effort to become energy independent by 2030. The state is currently one of the most oil-dependent states, using fossil fuels to meet about eighty-five percent of its energy needs. In May 2010, Maine Governor John Baldacci signed an ocean energy bill into law that set a goal by the state to produce 5 gigawatts of electricity, or more than twice the state's maximum current usage, from renewable ocean resources by 2030.[27]

The University of Maine's Advanced Structures & Composites Center, led by Dr. Habib J. Dagher, plans to deploy a one-third scale model turbine (100-foot tall at the hub) on a floating platform at the Monhegan Island test site near Port Clyde. The university will follow this by designing and constructing a full-scale turbine (300 feet tall at the hub) with 3 to 5 megawatts output in 2012-2014, with a goal to foster development of a 25-megawatt wind farm, consisting of five 5-megawatt floating turbines, erected ten to fifteen miles off the coast. Ultimately, the state foresees itself building 4,000 megawatts of offshore wind farm capacity by 2030. "That time frame allows us to learn how to build a wind farm in Maine by using Maine supply chain and Maine industry," Dagher told the *Morning Sentinel*, a Maine newspaper.[28]

The University of Maine's Advanced Structures & Composites Center, led by Dr. Habib J. Dagher (pictured), is poised to become the engineering epicenter for development and deployment of floating wind turbines off the U.S. Northeast coast.
Courtesy of University of Maine, Advanced Structures & Composites Center, Orono, Maine.

Mid-Atlantic

Not to be left out, the Mid-Atlantic coastal states of Delaware, Maryland, and Virginia have issued their own offshore wind energy proposals in recent years. Delaware has led the region with its approval in 2009 of developer NRG/Bluewater Wind's plan to construct a 450-megawatt offshore wind farm about 7.5 miles off Rehoboth Beach between the shipping lanes and Delaware Bay. "We do think that there is a real advantage to being early in a space like this rather than coming sort of into it too late when there is too many people trying to carve up the pie. We'd been coming to the conclusion before we approached Bluewater that offshore wind for the East Coast, especially the Northeast really makes sense, because it's one of the few

renewable resources that you can really build with scale and make a big enough scale to actually make them economic," said NRG Energy Executive Vice President Andrew Murphy at the time the company acquired Bluewater in November 2009.[29]

In April 2010, the Department of the Interior issued the nation's first initial request for interest for renewable energy development off the Delaware coast. In April 2009, the Obama administration announced the final framework for Outer Continental Shelf renewable energy development, which established a program to grant leases, easements, and rights-of-way for orderly, safe, and environmentally reasonable development of renewable energy. The new program, administered by the department's Minerals Management Service, also established methods for sharing revenues generated from Outer Continental Shelf renewable energy projects with affected coastal states.[30]

Although NRG/Bluewater has already entered a 25-year agreement to sell 200 megawatts of the wind farm's power to utility Delmarva, the developer must still apply to the Minerals Management Service for an offshore lease, which may entail competing with other companies if competitive interest exists. The agency will use industry responses to gauge specific interest in the commercial development of wind resources off the state's shores. If responses indicate there is no competitive interest in this area, the agency may proceed with the noncompetitive lease process.[31] NRG/Bluewater plans to start producing billable electricity by late 2013 or early 2014 from its Delaware offshore wind farm.

Last year, Lewes, Delaware, once a location for near-shore European-style windmills throughout the seventeenth and eighteenth centuries, became the home for a 2-megawatt near-shore wind turbine. The turbine is operated through the First State Marine Wind, a joint venture between the University of Delaware's Blue Hen Wind and Gamesa Technology.[32] The turbine is expected to generate more than enough power for the university campus at Lewes. The National Renewable Energy Laboratory will also work with the university to study turbine corrosion, bird interactions and policy issues related to renewable energy.[33]

In December 2009, Maryland released a report, *The Power of Offshore Wind: A Source of Clean, Reliable, Affordable Electricity for Maryland's Future*, which concluded that a wind farm off the state's Atlantic coast would help stabilize energy prices for Marylanders, who have seen more than a 75 percent increase in their electricity prices since 2002. The state has committed to reducing greenhouse gas emissions twenty-five percent below 2006 levels by 2020, and offshore wind could help achieve those reductions. "One offshore wind farm with 600 megawatts of generating capacity could prevent more than 2 million metric tons of global warming pollution per year, an amount equivalent to four percent of Maryland's emissions from electricity generation," the state declared.[34]

With the exception of the 50-megawatt Roth Rock wind farm installed in the western part of the state in 2010, Maryland's wind energy development on land remains largely constrained by geography and a public generally opposed to installing giant turbines on the state's western mountain ridges. About sixty percent of Maryland's electricity currently comes from coal-fired power plants, and the state imports almost one-third of its electricity from West Virginia and Pennsylvania. The Maryland Energy Administration believes that offshore wind development can help stabilize electricity prices, reduce the need for politically unpopular transmission lines, and help fight global warming.[35]

In 2009, Virginia announced the completion of a two-year study into the viability of a wind farm off the coast of Virginia Beach. The 67-page *Virginia Offshore Wind Studies, July 2007 to March 2010 Final Report*, conducted by the Virginia Coastal Energy Research Consortium, identified twenty-five Outer Continental Shelf lease blocks of Class 6 winds beyond twelve nautical miles offshore with water depths of less than 30 meters (100 feet) capable of supporting about 3,200 megawatts of offshore wind farm capacity.[36] The proposed offshore wind farm locations should also avoid interference with Virginia Beach's busy shipping channels and naval installation. The study's authors stated: "The greatest downside risk in our offshore wind energy cost estimates is the large uncertainty associated with the vertical distribution of wind speeds, which yield a standard deviation in the range of twenty to twenty-five percent in annual energy generation estimates at (turbine) hub height. This can be mitigated by an aggressive program of wind resource modeling validated by tall mast wind measurements."[37]

By early 2010, two Virginia companies had applied to the federal government to build offshore wind farms: Apex Wind Energy proposes to lease 116,000 acres to generate up to 1,500 megawatts and Seawind Renewable Energy Corp. wants to erect as many as 240 turbines offshore.[38]

However, Delaware, Maryland, and Virginia may have the best results of developing the Mid-Atlantic region's offshore wind potential by working together. On November 10, 2009, the governors of the three states entered a partnership to develop the region's offshore wind energy potential. The agreement calls for the states to:

• Identify common transmission strategies for offshore wind energy deployment in the region.
• Discuss ways to encourage sustainable market demand for offshore wind energy.
• Work together to pursue federal energy policies that help advance offshore wind power in the Mid-Atlantic.

"This agreement will help us leverage the resources and energy of our three state governments to help our region become the true powerhouse for this important source of renewable, reliable alternative energy," said Delaware Governor Jack Markell at the time of the agreement's announcement.[39]

South Atlantic

The South Atlantic states of North Carolina, South Carolina, and Georgia also have plans for harnessing the energy potential from their offshore winds.

Outer Banks Ocean Energy Corp. has proposed building a 200-megawatt offshore wind farm, or enough power for 42,000 homes, off the coast of North Carolina. The so-called Cape Lookout Energy Preserve will likely face intense public scrutiny, with transmission cables costing at least $2 million per mile to install over beaches, dunes and wetlands to reach the grid. If the approvals are secured, the developer said the earliest that power could be generated from the facility is 2014. The complete wind farm would consist of at least 150 turbines spread across 54-square-miles.[40] Duke Energy Corp., which is an experienced operator of land-based wind farms nationwide, announced in October 2009 that it would fund a pilot study into the feasibility of offshore wind energy production off North Carolina. The study, managed by the University of North Carolina at Chapel Hill, includes the erection of up to three wind turbines on Pamlico Sound.[41]

In South Carolina, the state-owned electric and water utility Santee Cooper is working with Coastal Carolina University and the state's Energy Office to assess the state's offshore wind potential. Previous research and mapping have determined that the state's onshore wind resources won't support commercial wind turbines, but there is potential for sustainable winds off the coast. Santee Cooper has deployed six buoys and two land-based stations to measure wind speed, direction, and frequency up to six miles off the South Carolina coast. One string of buoys begins at Georgetown near an ongoing coastal wind study at Winyah Bay, and the second string of buoys begins at Waites Island near an additional wind study at Little River. After sufficient buoy data is collected, Santee Cooper plans to install an offshore platform near one of the buoy paths to measure upper-level winds similar to those a wind turbine would encounter. The state's Energy Office will use the results to evaluate the feasibility of an 80-megawatt wind farm with twenty-two 3.6-megawatt turbines.[42]

Southern Company, a Georgia utility, commissioned Georgia Tech University to conduct a study of potential offshore wind energy sites ten miles off Tybee and Jekyll islands. The study, completed in 2008, found that wind energy off the Georgia coast was viable, but unaffordable to convert into electricity. Yet Southern Company has not dismissed offshore wind energy development and plans to install meteorological towers off Savannah to continue its wind research and has also considered doing similar research off the Florida panhandle.[43]

Gulf of Mexico

In recent years, Texas has catapulted to the forefront of U.S. wind farm development onshore with its abundance of wind-rich lands and minimal public resistance to large wind projects. The American Wind Energy Association calculated at the end of 2009 that Texas built 9,506 megawatts of wind farms, with another 352 megawatts under construction; followed by Iowa (3,670 megawatts), California (2,723 megawatts), Oregon (1,920 megawatts), and Washington (1,908 megawatts).[44] The state has been equally aggressive in its effort to exploit the wind resources off its coast. Texas has one of the most unusual coastal regulatory authorizes in the United States. While other states have rights over submerged lands up to three nautical miles off their coasts, Texas' authority stretches nine nautical miles, or three nautical leagues, from its coastline. This difference dates back to 1836 when the Republic of Texas won independence from Mexico. Texas entered the Union in 1845 with its offshore boundaries intact. Today, all offshore wind farm applications run through one state office — the Texas General Land Office — for approval, not multiple offices as is the case in most states.

Herman Schellstede and his business partner Harold Schaeffer, both engineers with four decades of experience in offshore oil and gas in the Gulf, have been at the forefront of offshore wind development in the region. In 2004, their firm Wind Energy Systems Technologies (WEST) proposed a plan to build a 50-megawatt wind farm near Grand Isle or Port Fourchon, Louisiana. The plan called for a network of twenty-three wind turbines built on a combination of existing oil and gas platforms, plus a series of small satellite platforms installed by WEST. Schellstede estimated at the time that the project would cost between $60 and $70 million and could use electric cables run through abandoned underwater oil pipelines to enter the landside power grid.[45] Of the more than 4,000 platforms operating in the Gulf, about 1,000 are within twelve miles from shore. Schellstede believes that offshore wind farm developers in the Gulf will face less public resistance to these projects than their brethren on the East Coast. "In Louisiana we've been accustomed to seeing lights out in the ocean so I don't think we'll have a public outcry," he told the *New Orleans City Business* newspaper in a September 2004 interview.[46] Yet this project appears to be on hold, while WEST has focused its recent attention on offshore wind farm endeavors on the Texas coast.

In 2005, the Texas General Land Office granted leases to WEST and Superior Wind Energy for projects off the coast of Galveston and South Padre Island, respectively. Superior Wind withdrew its project proposal shortly after citing economic concerns and a preference toward landside wind farm development.[47] WEST's lease calls for the development of a 150-megawatt wind park to be built on an 11,365-acre plot seven miles off the coast of Galveston. A year later, the state awarded Babcock & Brown Ltd. the rights to develop 39,000 acres of submerged lands off South Padre Island, south of Baffin Bay. This proposed wind farm would generate 500 megawatts of power, or enough to satisfy a small city or about 125,000 homes. Babcock & Brown withdrew its proposal in May 2007, stating that the project was not economically feasible.[48]

WEST uses a meteorological tower near Galveston to measure wind conditions in preparation for its future offshore wind farm. *Courtesy of Wind Energy System Technologies, New Iberia, Louisiana.*

These setbacks haven't stopped the Texas General Land Office from issuing other leases. In October 2007, WEST received an award for another four leases for offshore wind projects, in which the company has erected a meteorological tower for wind evaluation and has started conducting avian impact analyses. In July 2009, the Baryonyx Corporation of Texas was awarded a lease for two offshore wind concessions. The tracts for the offshore projects consist of 19,010 acres near Mustang Island and 19,794 acres off the coast from Rio Grande. According to the company, each project is supposed to generate wind energy in combination with other low-carbon energy production and storage technologies to power large land-side data centers.[49]

West Coast

The U.S. West Coast offers substantial commercial-grade winds for offshore wind farms. However, the Outer Continental Shelf along the coast, for the most part, quickly slopes to depths that render conventional seabed wind turbine foundations useless. In Northern California, there is a stretch of coastline with shallow water depths to support an offshore wind farm. In November 2008, Principle Power Inc. and the Tillamook Intergovernmental Development Agency proposed a demonstration project for a floating turbine off the coast of Oregon (see *Chapter 10*). Yet California, Oregon, and Washington remain focused on the development of large-scale landside wind farms.

Off the west coast of Canada, north of Vancouver, British Columbia, NaiKun Wind Energy Group has spent the past six years conducting environmental studies and community consultations to build a 396-megawatt offshore wind farm. In December 2009, the firm received its provincial Environmental Assessment Certificate from the British Columbia government, a significant hurdle past along the path toward starting construction. Currently, major hydroelectric generating stations on the Columbia and Peace rivers supply most of the province's electricity. The gap in energy is filled with imports of power from the United States and Alberta, generated by fossil fuels. The province's Energy Plan has a target of meeting and exceeding a goal of electric self-sufficiency by 2014.

The NaiKun offshore wind energy project will be located several kilometers off the coast of Haida Gwaii in the Hecate Strait, a passage that separates the Queen Charlotte Islands from the British Columbia coast. The site is known for its Class 7 winds, the highest in the U.S. Standard Wind Classification Scale. For NaiKun, the Hecate Strait is an ideal location for an offshore wind project due to its flat seabed, shallow water, and close access to a shore-side power grid. Up to 110 Siemens 3.6-megawatt wind turbines will be installed about one kilometer (just over a half mile) apart at a maximum of eight kilometers (five miles) off the east coast of Haida Gwaii, between Cape Ball and Rose Spit. Energy from the turbines will feed into an offshore converter platform in the middle of the project and be transmitted via sub-sea cable to Ridley Island, where it will be routed to BC Hydro's main power grid in Port Edward. Another proposed cable — the Haida Link — would connect to existing transmission lines on Haida Gwaii, with the landfall and substation near Tlell on Graham Island.[50]

The project suffered a setback in March 2010 when BC Hydro failed to accept NaiKun among its power purchase agreements — a final step for the offshore wind farm to go forward. NaiKun's board still believes that the wind farm could play a vital part of making British Columbia energy independent. In May 2010, the company restructured its operations to reduce costs and ensure financial resources to support the development of the offshore wind farm project into 2014.[51]

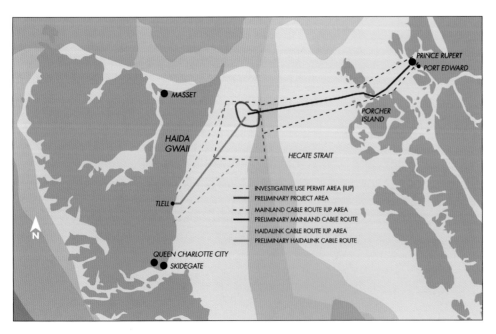

The NaiKun offshore wind energy project will be located several kilometers off the coast of Haida Gwaii in the Hecate Strait, a passageway that separates the Queen Charlotte Islands from the British Columbia coast. *Courtesy of NaiKun Wind Energy Group, Vancouver, British Columbia, Canada.*

Great Lakes

Offshore wind farms that will be distinct to North America are proposed by both U.S. and Canadian developers in the freshwaters of the Great Lakes. On the U.S. side, states leading this effort are Michigan, Wisconsin, Ohio and New York, while on the Canadian side Ontario is the primary province in this area. Wind resource studies show that the Great Lakes could effectively support large-scale offshore wind farms. The bi-national Great Lakes Wind Collaboration has spent the past several years attempting to clearly define offshore wind farm regulations and site strategies. For example, while the Minerals Management Service is the lead agency for approving wind farms in federal coastal waters, in the U.S. Great Lakes that authority is under the jurisdiction of the Army Corps of Engineers through Section 10 of the Rivers and Harbors Act and Section 404 of the Clean Water Act. This hasn't stopped the individual U.S. states and Canadian provinces in the Great Lakes region from pursing wind energy studies and considering proposals for offshore wind farms.

In 2008, the Michigan State University Land Policy Initiative studied the wind potential for the Great Lakes and found that about 100,000 turbines off Michigan's coast could produce 321,000 megawatts of energy. Michigan contains within its jurisdiction about forty percent of the Great Lakes Water surface area. The study did not take into account the state's many coastal use restrictions and environmental protections, which would preclude the unfettered construction of offshore wind farms.[52]

In 2009, Scandia Wind Offshore and Havgul Clean Energy proposed building a 1,000-megawatt wind project with one hundred to two hundred turbines of 5 to 10 megawatts each in Lake Michigan starting at two to four miles from shore at the Oceana-Mason county line and spread across an estimated 100-square-miles. The initial site for the Aegir Offshore Wind Farm was a good choice for the developers because of the relatively shallow water depths and its close proximity to the transmission lines at the Ludington Pumped Storage Plant, which feed electricity into the Chicago and Milwaukee markets.[53]

However, the developers, especially Havgul, a developer of onshore and offshore wind farms in Europe since 1995 and the developer of the massive Mariah Wind Power project in the Texas panhandle, weren't prepared for the level of public backlash against the Lake Michigan project. By early 2010, the companies decided to cut the size of the project in half and eliminate the southern end of the proposed site to move it further from the Silver Lake State Park shoreline.[54] Michigan coastal areas most conducive to offshore wind farms may be along its northeast coast in Lake Huron and the coasts of the upper-peninsula since these sites are less populated, thus less objectionable to the sight of offshore wind turbines.[55]

A 2004 study funded by the Wisconsin Focus Energy Program found promising wind activity along the state's southeast coast with Lake Michigan. Steady winds of 19 mph have been clocked in the area within a few miles from shore.[56] In April 2008, the Wisconsin Public Service Commission voted to study whether offshore wind turbines could be installed in Lake Michigan and Lake Superior. The commission study, released on January 15, 2009, found that wind energy would go a long way to help the state meet its proposed twenty-five percent renewable portfolio standard by 2025. While the study found offshore wind farms technically feasible, numerous economic, environmental and legal issues still stand in the way of efficient development.[57]

In Ohio, the Cuyahoga County Department of Development is leading an effort by the state to become a regional hub for the development of the Great Lakes offshore wind industry. Since 2007, the Cuyahoga County has touted wind energy as a means to jumpstart the state's industry and employment. In May 2009, the county released the results of a feasibility study performed on its behalf by German energy consulting firm juwi GmbH for the development of a five 20-megawatt pilot offshore wind energy project in Lake Erie near downtown Cleveland and associated test, certification, and advanced research centers. The area investigated for the pilot project is three to five miles from shore. The study identified nine potential turbine configurations at different locations in the project area. Based on established siting criteria, including water depth, geology, shipping lanes, underwater features, air navigation, radar, ecological concerns, and wind resources, the study recommended an area east of the Cleveland water intake Crib, about three miles from shore. The study found no "red flags" in respect to long-term disruption to marine ecology or avian species. According to the study, ice is expected to be the "principal design driver" for offshore wind turbines, which would be installed on monopile foundations. The county's summary of the report's ice evaluation stated:

> "It is assumed that an ice cone will be integrated into foundation design to break up ice at the waterline, reduce loading on the structure and avoid or minimize ice induced vibrations. The cone should be designed as an inverted ice cone where upper diameter is greater than lower diameter. Final design of the ice cone may require ice modeling in a cold weather laboratory, however ice is not identified as a prohibiting factor for wind turbines in the project area."[58]

In late 2009, Cuyahoga County's effort evolved into a new non-profit Lake Erie Development Corp. (LEEDCo.). In May 2010, LEEDCo. reached an agreement with General Electric to supply five 4-megawatt turbines specifically designed for offshore environments. The turbines will incorporate direct-drive technology gained through GE's acquisition of ScanWind in Sweden.[59] In addition to the 20-megawatt project off Cleveland in 2012, LEEDCo. and GE will collaborate on a strategic plan with the long-term goal of 1,000 megawatts in Ohio waters of Lake Erie by 2020.[60]

New York has also committed to developing offshore wind farms in the Great Lakes. In December 2009, the New York Power Authority announced a proposed plan to build wind turbines in state waters of Lake Erie or Lake Ontario. In specific, the power authority has requested

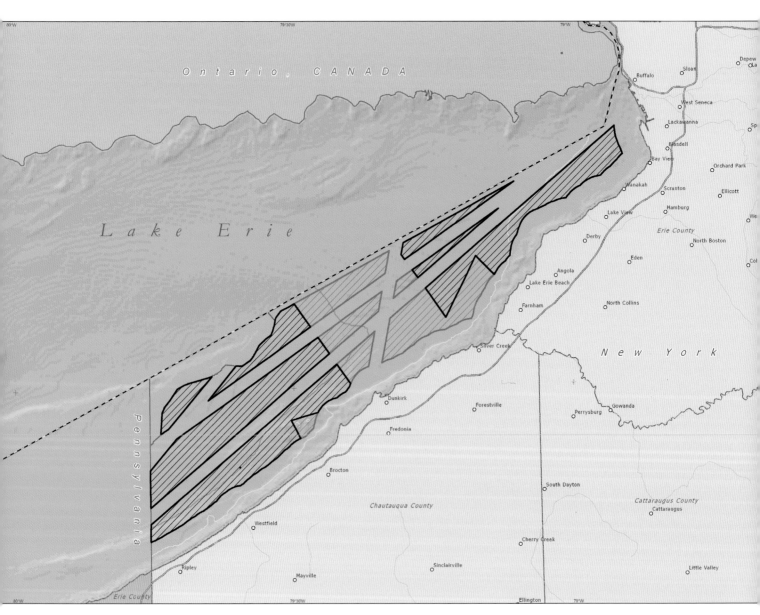

In December 2009, the New York Power Authority announced a proposed plan to build wind turbines in the state waters of Lake Erie or Lake Ontario in the range of 120 to 500 megawatts. *Courtesy of the New York Power Authority, White Plains, New York.*

proposals to develop a utility-scale offshore wind project in the range of 120 to 500 megawatts. The site selection identified thirteen potential areas in Lake Erie and ten areas in Lake Ontario. The project would interconnect with new or existing transmission facilities on shore and the power authority would buy the complete electric power from the project under a long-term power purchase agreement. An award will be made and the purchase agreements concluded by May 31, 2011, the power authority said.[61]

One of the more ambitious Great Lakes offshore wind farm developers is Toronto-based Trillium Power Wind. In mid-2009, the Canadian company proposed to build more than 3,600 megawatts of wind energy in the region. Trillium has already started developing its first project: a 710-megawatt wind farm in Lake Ontario, known as Trillium Power Wind I. This will be followed by three additional projects, including the 1,600-megawatt Great Lakes Array, the 650-megawatt Superior Array, and the 740-megawatt Trillium Power Wind II. The projects will be on the Canadian side of the Great Lakes and more than six miles from shore. The company's preliminary cost estimate for the three additional projects in 2009 was $8 billion, excluding transmission costs. The projects are eligible for a 19 Canadian cents per kilowatt-hour (U.S. 17.4 cents) feed-in tariff enacted for offshore wind farms by the Ontario government. Trillium Power Wind I was announced three years ago and will be located seventeen miles from the mainland of Prince Edward County, Ontario. The company hopes to complete construction of the first wind farm in 2013 or 2014, with the other three installed in phases over the next decade.[62]

However, the Great Lakes offshore wind farms will be challenged by opponents on both sides of the border. In April 2010, the community of Evanston, Illinois, rejected a plan to build an offshore wind farm.[63] These types of negative reactions will make it difficult for Great Lakes developers to carve out their place in the North American offshore wind energy industry. John Kourtoff, president and chief executive officer of Trillium, echoed this frustration in an August 2009 statement:

"The Great Lakes should not be looked upon as some back water environment. From an engineering perspective, it is far less challenging to build in the Great Lakes [than the ocean]. It is surprising that there is a lack of understanding of the unique opportunities; the silence has been deafening."[64]

Vessels and Ports

Offshore wind energy may be one of the most promising sources of clean electric power generation for North America in the next five to ten years, but enabling construction of these major projects to begin will be no easy feat. Port infrastructure and vessel equipment need to be built that specifically cater to efficiently handling these large-scale offshore projects.

Vessel operators and shipyards that have been engaged for more than thirty years in the U.S. offshore oil and gas sector are keeping a close eye on the prospects of contributing to the construction and maintenance of future offshore wind farms. However, there's a concern among developers whether there will be sufficient vessels once the wind farms begin full-scale development. In the United

States, offshore wind farm developers must comply with the U.S.-flag vessel requirements of Section 27 of the 1920 Merchant Marine Act, better known as the Jones Act, which may further test available ship capacity and raise installation costs. In addition to installation vessels, U.S. offshore wind farm operators will require fleets of maintenance vessels to transport parts and personnel safely and efficiently to the turbines.[65]

Industry analysts also note that efficiently managing turbine components and the vessels that transport them will require the development of coastal hub ports to serve regional clusters of offshore wind farms. Several ports in the U.S. Northeast are vying for the opportunity. In February 2010, Rhode Island's Quonset Development Corporation received a $22.3 million Transportation Investment Generating Economic Recovery (TIGER) grant from the U.S. Transportation Department, which will go toward helping reinforce the pier, purchasing a mobile crane capable of lifting up to 200 tons, and widening some roads between the port and two Deepwater Wind production and staging properties each about a half-mile away. The port may not only assist Deepwater's work off Rhode Island, but could also serve the interest of other offshore wind farm developers as far north as Maine and as far south as New Jersey.

The key to adequate port infrastructure is sufficient land to handle large wind turbine components, heavy cranes for lifting and relative close proximity to the major offshore sites. In January 2010, the Virginia Offshore Wind Coalition was formed by a group of developers, manufacturers, utilities and environmental groups with a central goal to promote Hampton Roads as a hub for manufacturing and supply for offshore wind farms in the region.[66] Some port facilities will also offer opportunities to test future offshore wind turbine technologies. Service Marine Group entered an agreement with Port Corpus Christi in Texas to acquire 916 acres, a significant portion of which was once part of the U.S. Naval Station Ingleside, to develop a wind and offshore renewable energy technologies development and test center, which is in line with research in this area by Texas A&M University System.[67]

Moving Forward

Many more projects will surely be announced along the East and West coasts and in the Great Lakes in the years ahead. In the United States, the goal is to generate twenty percent of electric power from wind (246 gigawatts on land and 54 gigawatts offshore) by 2030. How the North American offshore wind energy industry will evolve in the next five to ten years will depend on the strength of the regional economy, competitive pricing with fossil fuels, political will, stable government incentives, and public acceptance. U.S. wind project developers, both onshore and offshore, depend heavily on the longevity of the nation's production tax credit, which is similar in nature to Europe's feed-in-tariff. The PTC is essentially a federal rebate on the taxes paid by companies that own wind projects and helps wind farms become cost competitive with traditional fossil fuel-fired power plants. Onshore wind farm projects and investments have suffered routine delays in the United States over the years due to frequent lapses by Congress to renew the PTC. The current PTC is in place until 2012. To support the long-term nature of offshore wind projects, however, some industry analysts believe that the PTC should be extended for five to ten years at a time.[68]

Another way to improve sustainability of individual offshore wind projects in North America may be to connect them together by transmission lines. A University of Delaware study noted: "Each individual wind power generation site exhibits the expected ups and downs. But when we simulate a power line connecting them, called here the Atlantic Transmission Grid, the output from the entire set of generators rarely reaches either low or full power, and power changes slowly."[69]

On June 8, 2010, the states of Maine, New Hampshire, Massachusetts, Rhode Island, New York, New Jersey, Delaware, Maryland, Virginia, and North Carolina entered into a memorandum of understanding with the Department of the Interior to form the Atlantic Offshore Wind Energy Consortium, designed to coordinate regional promotion and development of offshore wind power.[70]

Chapter Seven

Global Opportunities

The first offshore wind farm outside of Europe was built in the shallow waters near the northern Japanese town of Setana in Hokkaido in 2003. The two Vestas 600-kilowatt turbines were erected 700 meters (about a half mile) offshore in 11 meters (thirty-six feet) of water. The turbines generate enough power a year for about 1,000 average-sized homes. Summit Wind Power constructed another larger offshore wind project that year at Sakata in Akita. This near-shore wind farm consists of five Vestas 2-megawatt turbines for a total rated capacity of 10 megawatts.[1]

In 2003, the Japanese government introduced a renewable portfolio standard with the goal to provide 3,000 megawatts of wind energy, both onshore and offshore, to the country's electrical supply in 2010, and a goal to reduce greenhouse gas emissions by six percent from 2008 to 2012. However, Japan's wind energy program has largely failed to meet these objectives, with only 1,880 megawatts of onshore and offshore wind turbines installed by 2008. Offshore wind, in specific, has been hampered by technical challenges associated with deep water surrounding the Japanese islands and the government's failure to sufficiently fund research and development efforts. Japanese fishermen, concerned about their water usage rights, have protested the construction of offshore wind farms[2], and Japan's grid infrastructure continues to pose an obstacle for many wind projects.

According to both the Japanese Wind Energy Association and Japanese Wind Power Association, the best wind energy sites are located in the remote northern and southern regions of the country, whereas the best grid connections and bulk of consumer demand are found in central Japan. Also, the country's frequent encounters with powerful storms have dampened wind energy's momentum. In 2003, Typhoon Maemi damaged all six turbines of the wind farm on Miyakojima Island near Okinawa. The storm's 90 meters-per-second (near 200 mph) wind gusts bent the towers of two turbines, pulled up the foundation of a third, and snapped the blades off the rest.[3]

Japan began construction of the concrete foundations for its second offshore wind farm in 2003 at the Sakata port in Akita.
Courtesy of Hikaru Matsumiya, Tokyo, Japan.

Five offshore Vestas 2-megawatt turbines in operation at Sakata port in Akita.
Courtesy of Hikaru Matsumiya, Tokyo, Japan.

Residents enjoy fishing under the offshore turbines at Sakata port.
Courtesy of Hikaru Matsumiya, Tokyo, Japan.

However, Japan has not given up on its offshore wind power aspirations. In late 2009, construction of the Kamisu offshore wind farm at Ibaraki got underway and will include seven 2-megawatt Subaru (downwind) units installed on monopile foundations about 40 meters (132 feet) from shore. Offshore wind and wave energy studies continue, in addition to consideration of wind turbines that will float in deep water. Since 2008, Tokyo Electric Power Co. and the University of Tokyo have studied the possibility of establishing large-scale floating wind farms.[4]

Japan's offshore wind energy potential may ultimately rest on the success that its turbine developers have with participating in projects in overseas markets, such as Europe and North America. In early 2010, Mitsubishi Power Systems Europe Ltd., a division of Mitsubishi Heavy Industries (MHI), entered a memorandum of understanding with the British government to invest up to 100 million pounds ($150 million) to engage in the development of supersize offshore wind turbines. In specific, Mitsubishi plans to test a 6-megawatt unit and, at its U.K.-based Offshore Wind Center for Advanced Technology, develop even larger and more sophisticated turbines. MHI's Ship Building division also expressed interest in entering Europe's offshore wind installation and operation and maintenance vessel markets.[5]

In 2009, Japan began construction of the Kamisu offshore wind farm at Ibaraki, consisting of seven 2-megawatt Subaru (downwind) units.
Courtesy of Hikaru Matsumiya, Tokyo, Japan.

China

In November 2007, China National Offshore Oil Corp. erected a test wind turbine on its Bohai Suizhong 36-1 oil platform, 70 kilometers (forty-four miles) off the coast, making it China's first foray into offshore wind energy. The 1.5-megawatt turbine, which was built by Xinjiang Goldwind, generates an estimated 4.4 million kilowatt hours of electricity a year for the platform.[6]

In May 2010, China constructed its first offshore wind farm 8 to 10 kilometers (five to six miles) off the coast in the Yangtze River Delta near Shanghai's Donghui bridge. The 102-megawatt project, which uses thirty-four 3-megawatt wind turbines manufactured by Sinovelwind Co. Ltd. of China, marks the start of what is expected to be a massive offshore windpower development effort by the country. Since 2005, the Chinese government has implemented a number of measures to stimulate and maintain its wind power sector. These programs include tax incentives for developers, fixed standardized electricity rates and domestic manufacturing requirements. China promulgated its Renewable Energy Mid- and Long-Term Plan two years later. Since then, China has entered a stage of rapid development in windpower.[7]

In addition to its immense political will, China also has an abundant wind resource both on land and offshore. China's Meteorological Administration estimates the onshore wind resource to be 600 to 1,000 gigawatts, while offshore winds offer between 100 and 200 gigawatts.[8] Similar to United States, China's most fertile wind resources are found in the interior. Thousands of miles of power lines must be run from these distant wind farms to population centers along the eastern seaboard. The Chinese Wind Energy Association reported at the end of 2008 that 239 wind farms were constructed in China with a total installed capacity exceeding 12,000 megawatts, which placed the country at No. 4 in the world's wind energy rankings. However, the 6,000 megawatts of installed capacity alone in 2008 made China the second largest wind energy producer in the world. Nearly all this installed capacity has so far been on shore.[9]

China's coastal provinces now want to exploit their offshore wind resources. In January 2010, the central government in Beijing signaled its priority to develop large-scale offshore wind farms, and placed two agencies in charge of the effort. The National Energy Administration oversees offshore planning and project approvals, while the State Oceanic Administration supervises issues related to marine environmental protection and the use of marine areas. Offshore wind farm developers will be selected through a rigorous public tender process with consideration of offered prices to send power to grids, technical capacity and performance results. These developers must also be Chinese-funded enterprises or fifty percent controlled Chinese joint ventures.[10]

In May 2010, China built its first offshore wind farm off the coast of the Yangtze River Delta near Shanghai's Donghui bridge. The 102-megawatt project consists of thirty-four 3-megawatt wind turbines manufactured by Sinovelwind Co. Ltd.
Courtesy of the Chinese Wind Energy Association, Beijing, China.

In February 2010, the National Energy Administration asked eleven provinces — Liaoning, Hebei, Tianjin, Shanghai, Shandong, Jiangsu, Zhejiang, Fujian, Guangdong, Guangxi, and Hainin — to submit their potential offshore projects for national tendering. Jiangsu, north of Shanghai, is one of the most promising provinces for offshore wind farms, with its strong winds and extensive tidal flats. By early 2010, a 30-megawatt project by Longyuan Group and a 6-megawatt by China Three Gorges were underway at Jiangsu; these were followed by an announcement from China's largest coal producer Shenhua Guohua Energy Investment to build two 300-megawatt offshore projects.[11]

Under the Chinese government's 2010 Interim Measure on the Management of Offshore Wind Farm Development, the first offshore concessions are expected to target projects of at least 100 megawatts in size, and up to 200 and 300 megawatts each. The agency has even requested assessments for projects in the range of 1 gigawatt.[12] Azure International, a Beijing-based energy consultancy, estimated that China could install up to 514 megawatts of offshore wind projects by 2014 and 2015. By 2020, the firm predicted that China's investment in offshore wind would reach $100 billion with up to 30,000 megawatts of output.[13]

China's turbine manufacturers are already preparing for the potential boon in offshore business. Sinovel has its 3-megawatt turbine in operation offshore of Shanghai and was scheduled to start manufacturing a 5-megawatt version late last year. Dongfang Turbine Co. Ltd. began producing a 5-megawatt offshore turbine in 2010, and Goldwind tested a 2.5-megawatt offshore unit for full production in October of last year. Shanghai Electric, CSIC, XEMC, and United Power are other Chinese companies with the existing technology or have plans to build offshore wind turbines in the range of 2 to 3 megawatts by early 2011.[14]

According to the Massachusetts Institute of Technology's April 5, 2010 *Technology Review*: "A key technical challenge is engineering for the tidal flat's muddy seafloors and shifting sandbars, which require different foundations and installation vessels than those developed for [Europe's] North Sea. Guohua, for example, is developing a novel steel pile foundation for its Jiangsu wind farms. Rather than the single steel monopiles common for North Sea projects, Guohua's will employ five piles, each 56 meters (184 feet) long."[15]

Hong Kong has considered the potential of offshore wind energy for more than a decade due to its scarcity of space to build landside wind farms and immense energy use. Scientists estimate that Hong Kong has an offshore wind capable of generating 25-terawatt hours of electricity, or enough to cover seventy-two percent of the Chinese territory's annual power consumption at 1998 levels.[16]

However, Hong Kong's dense ocean shipping lanes preclude it from taking full advantage of its offshore winds.

A 2000 study hypothetically proposed that a wind farm set up within an offshore space of 24 x 11 kilometers (15 x 7 miles) on the east side of the territory could generate as much as 2.1-terawatt hours, or six percent of Hong Kong's 1998 power demand.[17]

Hong Kong's efforts in wind energy, however, have progressed little. Hong Kong Electric Co. erected its first wind turbine on Lamma Island in early 2006. The turbine is capable of generating 800 kilowatts of power. In 2009, CLP Holdings Ltd., Hong Kong's largest power supplier, was granted permission by the territorial government to explore the development of a 200-megawatt offshore wind farm, which would produce enough power to meet one percent of the city's electricity. CLP plans to have wind and wave data for the project collected and analyzed by 2011. Even with further government approvals, the wind farm is not likely to be operational before 2014.[18]

Taiwan

Not far from mainland China, the island of Taiwan has signaled its own offshore wind energy ambitions. Onshore, Taiwan suffers from land restrictions and generally low wind speeds. The best sites offshore for wind farm development are located along Taiwan's west-central coast and around the Penghu Archipelago.[19] The Taiwanese government implemented the Renewable Energy Act in July 2009, which requires the country to meet fifteen percent, or 8,450 megawatts, of its electricity demand from renewable energy sources by 2025. The government believes offshore windpower could meet at least 3,000 megawatts of this target.[20]

In October 2009, Taiwan Generations Corp. entered an agreement with Scotland-based energy company SeaEnergy Renewables to build a 600-megawatt wind farm off Taiwan's west coast. The Changhua offshore wind farm will be located about 2.5 to 10 kilometers (1.5 to six miles) from the Changhua county shoreline in water depths up to 30 meters (100 feet). SeaEnergy delivered the world's first deepwater wind farm — the 10-megawatt Beatrice offshore wind farm — in Europe. The company erected two 5-megawatt wind turbines in water depths of 45 meters (148 feet).[21]

South Korea

The Korean peninsula's west coast winds have also attracted increased attention. The South Korean government has encouraged the installation of landside wind farms since the 1997-98 financial crisis. The government aims to have upwards of 2,250 megawatts of windpower installed by 2012, but, like Japan, South Korea suffers from a lack of adequate roads and power grids that can reach into the windy mountainous areas of the country. Thus South Korea's interest in its offshore wind resources has increased in recent years. It's estimated that the country's offshore energy potential is about 4.6 gigawatts.[22] Encouraged by these prospects, Doosan Heavy Industries & Construction, a South Korean firm, began testing a 3-megawatt offshore wind turbine near the island of Jeju, with an aim to make it market-ready by 2012. The country's top shipyards, such as Hyundai Heavy Industries and Daewoo Shipbuilding & Marine Engineering, made announcements in 2009 to enter the offshore wind-turbine manufacturing business.[23] In early 2010, the South Korean government announced plans to test scores of wind turbines in the West Sea by 2012, with the intent of constructing large-scale offshore wind farms. An offshore wind farm in the West Sea is expected to start by generating 100 megawatts, with a potential build-out of 1 gigawatt.

"The rivalry is already very stiff for countries to stay ahead of the pack in offshore wind power generation. We also hope to gain a competitive edge through the wind farm in the West Sea," said Hwang Soo-sung, director of the Ministry of Knowledge Economy, in a February 7, 2010 *Korea Times* article.[24]

Across Asia

Other Asian countries, such as Australia, New Zealand, Vietnam, Indonesia, Malaysia, the Philippines, and India, are expected to embrace offshore windpower after assessing the economic and environmental benefits of projects already underway in the region. For example, by 2010, the Indian company Areva Renewables, the world's largest nuclear plant builder, had been involved in the construction of about 600 megawatts of offshore wind projects in Europe and estimates that it could build similar projects off India's west coast for thirty to forty percent cheaper.[25]

However, what's apparent, according to analysts, is that Asia, led by China and South Korea, will become a major player in offshore wind energy production and equipment manufacturing in the years ahead. A 2009 report by Emerging Energy Research predicts that the international offshore wind energy market will grow from $10 to $30 billion in the next decade.[26]

In 2009, energy consulting firm ODS-Petrodata Ltd. forecasted that global offshore windpower, currently under 2 gigawatts, will reach 55 gigawatts by 2020. In its report, *The International Offshore Wind Market to 2020*, the firm wrote that offshore wind turbine supply constraints will be overcome by existing giants, such as Siemens and Vestas, and several new European manufacturers during the next few years, but these firms will be eventually joined by Asian manufacturers, including South Korean conglomerates such as Hyundai and Daewoo, and at least ten Chinese firms.[27]

Chapter Eight

Small Offshore Wind

While much of the public's focus during the past twenty years has been on the spread of giant offshore wind turbines on the coasts, less noticeable, but largely present, on the seas is a host of small wind turbines used for various applications. Tens of thousands of these small turbines may be found today on the oceans affixed to moving and stationary offshore structures. Like the experimental electric power generating units used by the early Polar explorers (See *Chapter 1*), this technology was spun off during years of development of small land-based turbine designs.

Small wind turbine development for rural household and farm use started as a tinker's occupation in the early twentieth century. These early devices typically consisted of hand carved wooden "airplane type" blades attached to an automobile generator. Shortly after World War I, some industrious individuals with backgrounds in basic aerodynamics realized the financial potential for standardizing wind turbines to feed America's increasing desire for electricity to power radios and appliances. Farmers, who were located far away from the electric power grid of the cities and towns, would take their 6-volt radio batteries to town for charging at an auto repair shop, a task that cost them money and time away from work. The difference between these electric-power generating wind turbines and water-pumping windmills is in the design of the wind wheel. Earlier power-generating wind wheels used multi-bladed patterns. These wind wheels had high torque to pump water and were good at operating in low wind speeds, but the power output in higher winds was limited by the blocking action of the many blades themselves, known as "wind congestion."[1]

Windpower developers began taking interest in the sleeker propeller design used on early airplanes. The fewer propellers operating at high speeds allowed wind to flow through the swept area developing lift and efficiently harvesting the high-energy winds. These types of propellers, used in context of wind-based electricity generation, operate efficiently in average wind speeds ranging from 8 to 12 mph and are optimized for 20 to 25 mph where the most energy is typically available.[2]

Advertising from the late 1920s and early 1930s touted the benefits of commercially manufactured electric-generating wind machines to rural Americans. *Courtesy of Craig Toepfer, Chelsea, Michigan.*

INSTRUCTION BOOK

32 VOLT DIRECT DRIVE
Jacobs Wind Electric

IMPORTANT!
Read This Instruction Book
Before Your Plant is
Installed.

Operating Instructions
for proper care of your plant
and battery are in this book
KEEP and READ IT

THE JACOBS WIND ELECTRIC COMPANY, INC.
Minneapolis, Minnesota, U. S. A.

There's POWER In The AIR

32-Volt With your WINCHARGER 32-VOLT
MODEL 650-A

properly installed well above all
wind obstructions, you are
assured of dependable operation,
giving you the convenience of
electric light and power at
practically no operating cost or
attention.

Note: Read this booklet care-
fully in order to secure the
utmost satisfaction from your
Wincharger.

ASSEMBLY INSTRUCTIONS
WINCHARGER CORP.
SIOUX CITY, IOWA, U. S. A.
Keep This Book   Keep This Book

The industry that built the first commercially available small wind turbines emerged during the 1920s and 1930s in the U.S. Midwest. In response to the wildly successful farm electric plant industry dominated by Delco-Light, a division of General Motors, that brought electricity to farms across America, nearly two dozen manufacturers began competing in the farm electric market under names such as Wincharger Corp. of Sioux City, Iowa; LeJay Manufacturing in Minneapolis, Minnesota; Air Electric Machine Company in Spencer, Iowa; Parker–McCrory of Kansas City, Missouri; and Parris-Dunn in Clarinda, Iowa. These machines were available in 6-, 12-, and 32-volt models and could be found on metal towers throughout the U.S. and Canadian Great Plains.[3]

While many of the small early commercial radio models relied on blades made from a single 6-foot long, 1 x 4-inch spruce or fir board with a copper leading edge, a couple of makers believed this wasn't enough to generate windpower for the larger home appliances popularized by Delco-Light.[4] One of those firms was the Jacobs Wind Company, which was founded by brothers Joseph and Marcellus Jacobs in rural Montana in 1926 and established full-scale manufacturing operations in Minneapolis in 1929. After several years of testing, the Jacobs settled on a 14-foot diameter, three-bladed propeller constructed of high aircraft quality Sitka spruce from the U.S. West Coast. The Jacobs discovered that the three-bladed design prevented excessive vibration to the system whenever the wind shifted. In addition to smoother operation due to the aerodynamic and mechanical balance, the three-blade design started up easier in the wind because of a fifty percent increase in surface area over a comparable two-bladed propeller. Furthermore, the three-bladed rotor always returned to a static (no wind) position in which one blade is straight up and the two others are at equal points on both sides, thus exposing all the blades to unobstructed wind for startup.[5] Another successful manufacturer to grasp the three-bladed propeller, but with a downwind design and no tail (which was part of upwind designs), was the Wind Power Light Co. in Newton, Iowa, started by Ed McCardell and his father in 1932.[6]

While some Europeans developed their own small turbines, the United States remained the dominant manufacturer of these machines, exporting them all over the world for both home and industrial applications.

However, the U.S. industry started showing cracks in 1936 when Congress passed the Rural Electrification Act, which promised to extend electric power lines to rural Americans. By the mid-1950s, few remote farms and towns were without "high line" electric power from the cities. Farmers with farm and wind electric plants were often forced to remove or destroy their wind and farm electric equipment in order for the power companies to hook up to their properties. Thus many wind-turbine makers either disappeared from the market or turned to manufacturing other products. Parker-McCrory, for example, eventually became a maker of electric cattle fencing, Jacobs Wind closed its doors in 1956, and Wincharger and Wind Power Light Company transformed and merged and are operating today as Winco in Southern Minnesota.[7]

Interest in small turbines reemerged worldwide after the 1973 Arab oil embargo. The event emphasized American and European dependence on Middle Eastern oil, which during the panic shot up to $100 a barrel. The industrialized world also became more concerned about pollution. Suddenly, a market for reconditioned Jacobs and Winchargers took hold, of which many were still found in old barns and sheds on farms throughout the American Midwest. Entrepreneurs also surfaced on the market with promises to build affordable small wind machines for the average homeowner — some successful, many not.[8]

Early market leaders, such as Jacobs and Winco (formerly Wincharger), reentered the business with improved larger versions of their most successful models. In 1972, Marcellus Jacobs revived the Jacobs Wind Electric Company in Ft. Meyers, Florida and started working on a new wind turbine for modern needs. The company, which moved back to Minneapolis and was re-named Earth Energy Systems by their angel investor Control Data Corporation in 1980, produced a highly successful 20-kilowatt wind turbine and integrated it with a variety of industrial power applications. The Norman, Oklahoma-based Bergey Windpower Company, another promising wind turbine maker, entered the market in 1977 under the direction of Karl Bergey and his son Michael. After several years of testing, Bergey Windpower produced a three-bladed, 1-kilowatt turbine, followed by 1.5- and 10-kilowatt systems, for homes, farms, and small businesses.[9] By the early 1980s, there were about forty small turbine companies in the U.S. market, thriving off high oil prices, beneficial government regulations, and federal tax incentives.[10]

The U.S. industry would take a nosedive again in 1985, when Congress allowed the federal tax credit for small wind turbine companies to expire, and the Reagan administration showed little interest in continuing these types of alternative energy benefits. Another blow came with the steep drop in oil prices to about $10 a barrel. Many small wind turbine manufacturers exited the business. It was also the same year that Marcellus Jacobs died from injuries suffered in an automobile accident. A few companies, such as Bergey Windpower, survived, and some entrepreneurs, such as Andy Kruse and David Calley of Southwest Windpower in Flagstaff, Arizona, even entered the business in the 1980s. These companies found ways to reduce production costs in order to offer customers competitively priced products both in the United States and overseas, and they remain among the most recognized commercial names in small windpower today.[11]

Since the late 1990s, the market for small wind turbines, particularly in the United States, has reemerged with vigor as oil prices and electric utility bills started to rise. A host of new players have entered the small wind turbine market offering consumers non-traditional blade designs and promises of enhanced performance and electric power generation.

In the mid-1970s and through the ups and downs of the market for renewable energies, some small wind turbine makers successfully developed an offshore niche by offering their machines to operators of sailboats and oceangoing yachts. As Scott Dine wrote in his 2001 *Bay Weekly Online* article "Sailing off the Grid":

> "Electricity is in short supply on a sailboat, a sort of mini-California whose skipper is constantly trying to figure where the next watt will come from."[12]

Boat owners have increasingly outfitted floating living quarters with refrigerators, stoves, microwave ovens, stereos and televisions, power tools for making repairs, hot and cold-water pressure, electronic communications and navigation devices, and now computers, all of which require increasing amounts of electricity to operate. Sailboat operators have either relied on small gas and diesel engines to keep their 12-volt battery banks charged or shore-side chargers once the batteries are discharged. Small wind turbines offered sailors a remedy for steady battery charging.

Unlike in the United States, the United Kingdom had no history of widespread use of small stand-alone turbines for landside residential and commercial use. U.K. manufacturers sought and designed small wind machines for niche markets, which in this case was mainly the marine leisure market. Some of the earliest U.K. developers of sailing and yacht wind turbines are Ampair, AeroGen, and Marlec Engineering Co. Ampair described its yacht turbines as follows:

> "Ampair micro wind turbines are typically used for extended coastal cruising and to keep batteries topped up whilst a yacht is on the mooring, or berthed alongside. This reduces the need to run the main engines (which both cost diesel and maintenance; and are noisy) or to take an expensive marina power connection. This benefits weekend users who can return the yacht to mooring at the end of an intensive weekend trip, and leave it safe in the knowledge that the house and engine batteries will recharge during the week. Similarly coastal cruisers can make a trip of several weeks using anchorages and remote moorings without needing to become dependent on expensive or scarce marina berths. And lastly live aboard round the world cruisers can spend extended periods in remote anchorages with an absolute minimum of shore support."[13]

Sailors who embraced wind energy often found the best place to install these turbines was on top of poles at the stern, due to the limited topside space of sailboats and yachts.

A Bergey 50-kilowatt prototype wind turbine sits on top of a 120-foot monopole tower in front of a Wal-Mart store in McKinney, Texas, in June 2005. *Courtesy of Bergey Windpower, Norman, Oklahoma.*

Southwest Windpower released its popular swept-bladed Skystream 3.7 turbine in the summer of 2006. *Courtesy of Southwest Windpower, Flagstaff, Arizona.*

These early marine wind turbines generally started producing electricity in winds of about 7 knots. Beyond 35 knots, the machines had to be shut down to avoid overheating or overcharging and damaging the batteries.[14] The generators of the turbines needed to be properly sealed against the corrosive marine air. Early models also had the unsavory reputation of being noisy when their blades whipped in the wind. This was largely caused by the alternators of the machines having stator coils wound around steel punching. While these form the magnetic circuit in the machines, they also produce a series of hard spots as the alternator rotates. These hard spots are known as "cogging," which resonates as vibration when the turbine is operating at speed. Cogging is largely responsible for the thrumming noise experienced inside the yacht's accommodation. Vibration from the turbine travels down the mount tower and is transmitted through the yacht's deck and hull, much like the sound box of a guitar.[15] The aesthetics of the turbines are also difficult for some traditional yachtsmen to get past. Some turbine blades can easily reach five feet in diameter.[16]

Other small wind turbine makers entered the offshore market in the early 1990s with increasingly more efficient and aesthetically pleasing machines, such as Southwest Windpower's Air-X marine unit which incorporated a microprocessor to increase performance and improve battery charging, and a special blade design to reduce noise; and Windbugger in Fort Lauderdale, Florida, which promised a machine that self-starts in 6 knots of wind, generates a minimum of 0.5 amps, and in 25 knots of wind produces electricity at 18 amps or more. Some turbines were developed for the wind conditions of specific regional markets. In the mid-1990s, Canadian Doug Bills set up shop in Trinidad to build the KISS (Keep It Simple, Sailor) boat turbine for the Caribbean. One KISS user in 1998 described the turbine's 30-inch blades (for a 60-inch diameter rotor) as "a true airfoil, highly cambered and twisted near the hub for good low-speed torque. Blade ends are elliptical, minimizing tip noise — the annoying ripping sound that makes many wind generators such bad neighbors in an anchorage."[17]

The best place for marine turbines is in the trade wind areas, such as the Caribbean and the South Pacific islands, where the air's movement is more consistent and at a higher velocity. Like on land, ocean winds are fickle, and yacht operators making long ocean voyages often experience periods where winds are insufficient to turn turbine blades. To fix this problem, some marine turbine developers built so-called "hybrid" machines that are capable of being operated in either wind or water mode. Ampair's Aquair unit, developed in the mid-1990s, allowed the sailor to operate the unit in wind mode on a pole mount system, or detach it for submersion in the water.

According to Ampair, the conversion process takes no more than fifteen minutes. In water mode, the Aquair turbine is towed behind the boat on a 100-foot long rope attached to the stern railings. The company estimates that in the water its turbine generates about 1 amp per knot of boat speed,[18] but there are numerous disadvantages to traditional tow rope type water generators, including high drag, loss of boat speed, the tendency of the turbine to surface at high speeds, and generate fairly low power outputs (typically a maximum of 5 to 6 amps at 12 volts). These machines are awkward and inconvenient to deploy and recover. They prevent the yachtsman from deploying and trailing a fishing line and have reportedly become irresistible targets for predatory fish like sharks, resulting in many lost impellers.[19]

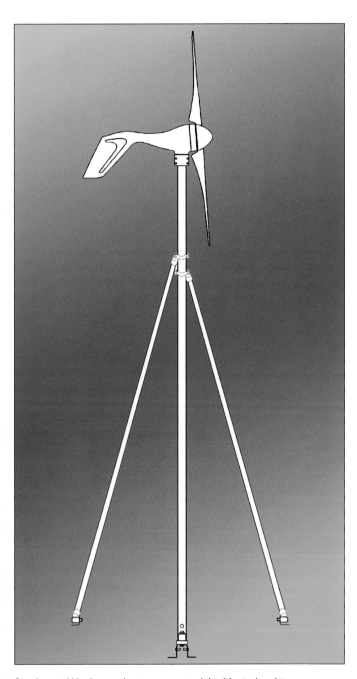

Southwest Windpower's stern-mounted Air-X wind turbine. *Courtesy of Southwest Windpower, Flagstaff, Arizona.*

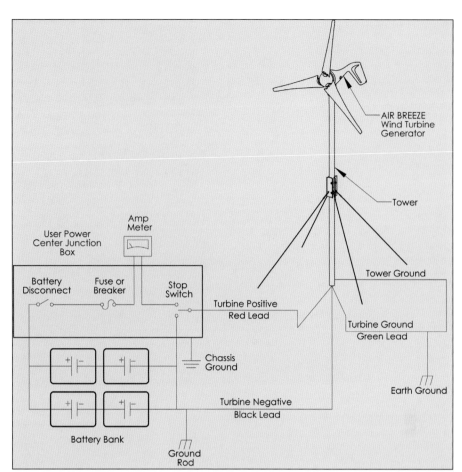

Wiring schematics for single and multiple small wind turbine setups. *Courtesy of Southwest Windpower, Flagstaff, Arizona.*

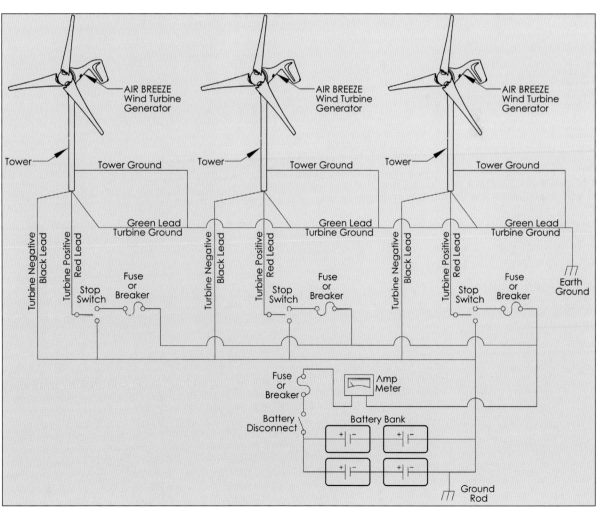

In the late 1990s, Pete Anderson, an avid sailor from the United Kingdom, set out to improve the operations and electric output of small wind/water turbines. After several years of design and testing, his company, Eclectic Energy Limited, introduced the DuoGen to the market in 2002. The first big difference between the DuoGen and its predecessors is the elimination of the tether. Based around a slow-speed 500-watt alternator, change between wind and water modes is achieved in seconds and without the need for tools. In water mode, the power produced at typical passage speeds of 5 to 6 knots is around 150 to 200 amp hours per day for a 12-volt system, which matches the electricity consumption of a typical blue water yacht. At anchor, or in harbor areas, the DuoGen's wind mode offers a powerful and quiet supplement.[20] The company estimates that more than 1,000 DuoGen units are in use today and, in many cases, they are the sole source of electrical power for yachtsmen on transatlantic and transpacific passages. Several DuoGens have completed full circumnavigations, and at least one machine is on its third time around.[21]

In the late 1990s, British sailor Pete Anderson set out to improve the operations and electric output of small wind/water turbines. He introduced the popular DuoGen to the sailing market in 2002, which provides ease and efficiency when switching between wind and water mode. *Courtesy of Eclectic Energy Ltd., Nottinghamshire, United Kingdom.*

In 2006, the company introduced an upgraded model, called the DuoGen-2. In addition, Eclectic Energy manufactures the D400 dedicated wind turbine that is also widely installed on yachts. Where an owner's sailing consists of shorter passages with extended periods in harbor or at anchor, the D400's wind performance and rugged "fit and forget" engineering makes it an attractive choice. Since the D400's alternator does not use iron with its windings, the machine emanates no annoying vibration above or below deck. So far, the company estimates that more than 1,600 D400s are now in service worldwide, with about fifty to sixty percent of them installed on sailboats and yachts.[22]

Small wind turbines may also eventually prove beneficial to large vessel operators. In 2004, Mitsui O.S.K. Line sought to test a turbine to introduce environmentally friendly technology on its vessels. Tokai University Research Institute of Science and Technology and Nishishiba Electric worked together with the carrier to develop and install an onboard, straight-wing, vertical axis-type wind power generator. The generator's compact shape and omni-directional rotation allowed it to generate power no matter which direction the wind blows. The device was installed on the *Taiho Maru's* bridge, where it received the strongest winds.[23] While the test was considered successful, MOL has no immediate plans to install turbines on its other vessels. MOL and Tokai University will continue to explore whether the turbine's electrical output could be sufficiently stabilized to power sensitive navigation and other ship-critical systems.[24]

In 2004, Japan's Tokai University Research Institute of Science and Technology and Nishishiba Electric worked together with Mitsui O.S.K. Lines to develop and test a straight-wing, vertical axis-type wind generator on-board one of the ocean carrier's ships.
Courtesy of Mitsui O.S.K. Lines, Tokyo, Japan.

In addition, oil platform operators have come to rely on electrical power generated by small wind turbines. It's estimated that nearly 500 platforms in the Gulf of Mexico use both small wind and photovoltaic panels to provide power for lighting and SCADA (supervisory control and data acquisition) systems that monitor the flow of oil and natural gas. In the Gulf, ExxonMobil and Kerr-McGee, for example, exclusively use Southwest Windpower's small wind generators for providing power on their offshore platforms, rather than consuming oil for thermal electric generators.[25] Small wind is often used rather than solar because solar panel arrays create large surface areas that result in wind loading off the platform.[26] Other offshore uses for small wind turbine-generated electrical power include monitoring stations for scientific and government organizations, signal platforms that help guide ships through shallow waters, and fish feeders (offshore fish farms).

A Southwest Windpower Air-X marine unit provides electric power to an offshore oil platform. *Courtesy of Southwest Windpower, Flagstaff, Arizona.*

Chapter Nine

Sea Battles

A new type of warfare is being waged on the sea over the placement of giant offshore wind turbines. Shots fired, in this case, are the rhetoric exchanges between those who either support or oppose this form of renewable energy. Both sides come armed with their own research and public relations spin in order to win followers and ultimately tip the battlefield in their favor. The fight is destined to be long, perhaps pinning neighbor against neighbor for years, and will likely leave a trail of hurt feelings no matter the outcome.

Nowhere in the United States has this been played out more than with Cape Wind's proposed wind farm at Nantucket Sound's Horseshoe Shoal off the coast of Cape Cod, Massachusetts. Since the inception of the project more than nine years ago, formidable camps of proponents and opponents have emerged on Cape Cod, each side taking ample shots at one another in the local and national press. The proponents, led by Cape Wind, cite the clean energy benefits of wind power. The shoal is considered one of the best locations for placing an offshore wind farm in the U.S. Northeast due to its ample wind, relatively shallow water depth, and proximity to a large coastal population. Cape Wind also spent more than $30 million since 2000 in environmental studies to ensure the wind farm's pre- and post-construction phases have no adverse impacts on birds, sea mammals, commercial and military aviation radar, local fishermen and tourism. "We've gone through a more rigorous evaluation process than any prior energy project in New England," said Jim Gordon, Cape Wind's president, in a 2008 interview with *Business Week*.[1] Even Massachusetts Governor Deval Patrick and the Obama administration have voiced strong support for Cape Wind.

Despite Cape Wind's positive attributes and the support for it, the opposition, led by the Alliance to Protect Nantucket Sound, has fought the project every step of the way. The alliance's ranks include some of Massachusetts' most powerful political and business figures, such as the late Sen. Edward Kennedy's family, heiress Bunny Milton, billionaire Bill Koch, and former state governor and presidential candidate Mitt Romney. Many in the alliance own pricey beachfront real estate on Cape Cod and do not want to see twirling wind turbines on the horizon. Speaking in the same 2008 *Business Week* article, Glenn Walthey, the alliance's chief executive officer, said the Cape Wind project "is like trying to put a wind farm in Yellowstone National Park as far as we're concerned."[2]

Just when it seemed like the battle was almost over and federal approval for Cape Wind was in sight, in late 2009 two Massachusetts Indian tribes requested that the entire 560-square-mile Nantucket Sound be listed on the National Register of Historic Places as a traditional cultural property. The tribes claim the wind farm would disturb their spiritual sun greetings and submerged burial grounds. During the last Ice Age, New England's coast extended more than seventy-five miles further into the sea, compared to the current shoreline.[3]

Lawmakers worldwide will generally listen to the anti-wind lobby as much as they do to the wind energy proponents. A split in opinions about the benefits of wind energy among politicians, federal and state agencies, and community activists may bog down wind projects for years and in some cases has resulted in abandoning projects altogether.

The media also plays an important role in influencing local decisions to either support or disapprove of a wind farm's construction. Unfortunately, newspapers and other media outlets tend to fortify their reporting around comments from celebrities and local personalities, inciting a "he said, she said" debate, rather than on the substantive environmental, social, and regulatory issues involving the projects.[4] This has largely been the case with the news reporting surrounding Cape Wind. The Alliance to Protect Nantucket Sound has used this tactic to its advantage, whereas the project's advocates "missed conveying a critical vision on how this one project could lead the U.S. into the future… that vision of the future might be one of the most important and compelling missing ingredients that would lead to more widespread support for projects such as this one."[5]

To avoid political gridlock or even a project's demise, it's important for wind farm developers not to ignore any potentially impacted party of a wind farm. Their efforts should include:

- Seeking resolutions with all parties that have concerns about a project.
- Evaluating the alternatives in the record.
- Avoiding temptations to take shortcuts.[6]

The opposition, when polled, is generally not opposed to wind energy, but object to the construction of these mechanical giants in their own backyard. Today's turbines are much better designed than the first generation of land-based machines from the 1970s and 1980s, which were known to be noisy and interrupt radio and television signals. Engineers have reduced the noise emissions through better tower and blade designs, and better antennae and receiver technologies have largely eliminated radio and television signal interference from onshore wind farms. Yet, it's impossible to escape the fact that turbines are large structures, and they continue to become even bigger, making visual-based opposition, both on land and at sea, still the top of the list.

Staring down a row of offshore wind turbines at the Burbo Bank offshore wind farm in the United Kingdom.
Courtesy of Wind Power Works, Global Wind Energy Council, Brussels, Belgium.

Visual impediments associated with wind turbines might be diminished by placing them farther away from population zones. For offshore wind farms, this means building turbines no closer than five miles from the shore.[7] In 2009, Santee Cooper, South Carolina's state-owned electric and water utility, together with Clemson University's South Carolina Institute for Energy Studies, developed a photo simulation that found while wind turbines may be visible with the human eye eight miles out from the state's Grand Strand shoreline, on a typical hazy summer day visibility will be reduced by half. The turbines used in the simulation are 3.6-megawatt models depicted with an offshore hub height of 328 feet and blades 164-feet long.[8] Manufacturers have also attempted to blend their turbines into the background of the sea by painting the towers, nacelle covers, and blades a light blue or gray color.[9] Unlike the U.S. East Coast and Great Lakes, people living along the Gulf of Mexico have witnessed offshore oil and gas platforms on the coastal horizon for more than thirty years and offshore wind farm developers there believe these populations will be less opposed to adding turbines to the mix. Yet, the farther wind farms are placed offshore, the higher the cost per kilowatt-hour will be for the electricity generated.[10]

To build an offshore wind farm just about anywhere in the world today requires developers to conduct numerous environmental impact studies before the first turbine can even be planted. The oceans team with life both above and below the water line, and these ecosystems could be negatively affected during the construction phase of an offshore wind farm, as well as during their long-term operation.

On the surface, offshore wind farm developers must consider the proximity of the site to commercial and military vessel navigation. Many coastal cities are built around active seaports. While vessel operators generally operate in designated channels upon entering and exiting ports, there is a need for sufficient buffer zones between vessels and fixed offshore structures during storms and other maritime emergencies. Even on the Great Lakes this is a significant issue for mariners. U.S. and Canadian vessel operators request a minimum three-mile safety zone along each side of the course lines.[11] It should be noted during the nearly two decades of operating offshore wind farms in Northern Europe, there were no reported boating accidents associated with these structures, and a number of these wind farms are built along some of the heaviest traveled shipping lanes in the world.[12]

Simulated photo shows how the 12-turbine Palmetto Wind offshore project off the coast of Little River might appear from a public beach in northern Horry County, South Carolina. The distance from shore to the turbines is 7.3 miles. Different light, wind and haze conditions could make them more or less visible. *Courtesy of Santee Cooper, Moncks Corner, South Carolina.*

Another simulated photo shows how the 40-megawatt Palmetto Wind offshore project placed off the coast of Winyah Bay, South Carolina, could appear from Debordieu, the closest populated area to the bay and about 8.7 miles from the proposed wind farm. The turbines are placed to match light and wind conditions at the time of the photo, which in this case decreased visibility. *Courtesy of Santee Cooper, Moncks Corner, South Carolina.*

Bird and marine mammal populations are generally monitored by national governments and intergovernmental organizations, as well as environmental groups. The biggest concern with wind turbines are birds impacting with spinning blades. A 2005-2006 study at the Danish offshore wind farms of Nysted and Horns Rev found that less than one percent of birds fly close enough to the turbines to risk collision. The same study witnessed some displacement of diving ducks at the sites. At the same time, researchers have discovered that turbines themselves have become resting places for cormorants and herring gulls.[13] Raptors may be the most vulnerable to offshore turbine collision due to their hunting habits. A near-shore wind farm at Smøla, Norway has been linked to high mortality and local population declines of white-tailed sea eagles that nest on the islands in the vicinity of the project.[14] The presence of the turbines may also cause some bird and marine mammal populations to avoid the area altogether.

U.S. offshore wind farm developers operating in federal waters are governed by the environmental assessment requirements of the National Environmental Policy Act and Federal Energy Policy Act, both enacted by Congress in 2005. Many types of birds and raptors and surface mammals are further protected from man-made harms under national laws including the Migratory Bird Treaty Act, Bald and Golden Eagle Protection Act, Endangered Species Act, and the Marine Mammal Protection Act. Each state also has its own coastal water environmental requirements. In the Great Lakes, the Army Corps of Engineers retains offshore wind project permitting authority, including environmental assessments, under Section 10 of the 1899 Rivers and Harbors Act. Numerous tools may be deployed in combination to better understand potential threats to birds and mammals within a proposed offshore wind farm site. These include routine seasonal visual assessments by aircraft, and the deployment of Doppler and tracking radar technologies. In 2010, scientists at the BioDiversity Research Institute implanted special satellite-based transmitters into four common eider ducks nesting in Maine's Casco Bay. Their goal is to track the offshore movement of the birds through the winter months to determine if they will be exposed to sites planned for floating wind energy projects.[15] Surface analyses and related technologies aimed at offshore wind farm environmental impacts to date are still in their infancy. A 2008 *Marine Technology Society Journal* article stated:

> "Research that better establishes the relationship between pre-construction activity and post construction impact is needed, but in the absence of reliable risk indicators regulators will need to make permitting decisions with criteria that use the best available scientific information, design mitigation on the basis of preconstruction assessments, and employ adaptive management that incorporates new information as it becomes available."[16]

Underwater environmental analysis is equally important during pre- and post-construction of offshore wind farms. How are fish populations affected by the acoustic and equipment activity associated with turbine foundation and sub-sea cable placements? Offshore wind farm developers say fish kills from these activities are minimal to non-existent, because fish will generally scatter to safer distances. Once these wind farms are built, fish have been noted to quickly return to the sites. Rocks placed around turbine foundations to prevent erosion have become artificial reefs. A U.K. offshore wind farm at Whitstable, Kent has witnessed the return of native oysters and mussels to the area, and a wind farm at North Hoyle, United Kingdom has become a favorite spot for sport fishing boat operators.[17]

Birds fly in range of the blades of a wind turbine.
Courtesy of the Renewable Energy Center, Saint Francis University, Loretto, Pennsylvania.

Offshore wind farm development has also contributed to its share of underwater archeological findings. In 2003, during the construction of Denmark's Nysted I offshore wind farm, workers found a large wooden rudder believed to be from the British warship *HMS St. George*, which lost the rudder in 1811. The rudder was raised and placed in the Stranding Museum at Thorsminde, Denmark.[18] In 2009, at Denmark's Rødsand II offshore wind farm site, builders located four historic anchors of unknown origin.[19] Offshore wind farm developers in the North Sea are instructed to watch for signs of submerged Stone Age villages.[20] It's believed that the offshore site, known as Doggerland, once was a land bridge connecting Britain to mainland Europe, but it sank into the North Sea about 8,000 years ago during the end of the last Ice Age.

There are also concerns about offshore turbine placements disturbing shipwrecks and unexploded ordnance. For example, the Horns Rev I offshore wind farm is built over the site of numerous known shipwrecks, including the fleet of German MTBs sunk when they struck their own mines in World War II. Extensive ordinance searches were conducted in the Kentish Flats of the Thames Estuary before any turbines were erected there, since it was known that thousands of bombs were dropped in the area during World War II. The U.K. and German coasts remain a big concern for offshore wind farm developers with the potential for unexploded ordinance on or below the seabed.[21]

In 2003, the lost rudder of the 1811 British warship *HMS St. George* was recovered during construction of the Danish Nysted I offshore wind farm.
Courtesy of the Stranding Museum, Thorsminde, Denmark.

Chapter Ten

Floating Wind Turbines

"If we're not willing to put the turbines up where the winds are, we might as well forget about wind power," declared William E. Heronemus, the University of Massachusetts professor who promoted the concept of offshore wind energy in the early 1970s, during an interview with *National Geographic* in 1975.[1]

That statement holds true today for many forward-thinking wind energy proponents. By 2020, it's realistic to expect that much of the suitable land and outer continental shelf, especially in North America and Europe, for wind farms will be exhausted, and the amount of energy produced at that point will still be a dent in the world's efforts to supplant fossil fuels for electric power production. Yet there remain significant opportunities for further wind power development in deeper waters offshore, or at depths of more than 60 meters (100 feet). Since 2005, more than a dozen universities, research laboratories, engineering firms, and wind turbine manufacturers throughout the world have explored concepts of floating turbines for deepwater deployment. The most productive winds are generally found 20 kilometers (12.5 miles) or farther offshore. Twenty-five percent increases in wind speed offshore will double a turbine's power generation while a fifty percent higher average wind speed will create a threefold increase in power.

Another factor driving wind turbines farther offshore is public complaints about visual impacts. "The next frontier of wind energy will feature multi-megawatt floating wind turbines deployed in gigawatt scale offshore wind farms placed at a distance from the coastline where tall towers are invisible and in water depths up to several hundred meters," wrote Paul Sclavounos, a professor with the Massachusetts Institute of Technology's Department of Mechanical Engineering in the *Marine Technology Society Journal* in 2008.[2] MIT and the U.S. Department of Energy's National Renewable Energy Laboratory have studied the concept of floating wind turbines in the capacity range of five megawatts since 2006.

In January 2007, the University of the Aegean in Greece launched a floating platform with a 30-kilowatt turbine, coupled with a photovoltaic system, to supply electricity to an onboard desalination unit to turn saltwater into potable water. The water is pumped by pipe from the floating platform to the island shore.
Courtesy of the Department of Shipping Trade and Transport, University of the Aegean, Chios, Greece.

The credit for launching the first floating wind turbine goes to the Department of Shipping Trade and Transport at the University of the Aegean in Chios, Greece. In January 2007, the university dispatched a floating platform with a 30-kilowatt wind turbine, coupled with a photovoltaic system, to supply electricity to an onboard desalination unit to turn saltwater into potable water. The desalinated water collects in a 25-cubic-meter (884 cubic feet) on board water tank and from there is pumped through a submerged pipe to a shore connection where it's stored in tanks on islands where fresh water is scarce. The floating platform of the test unit measures 20 x 20 meters (66 x 66 feet) and includes five metallic flotation cylinders. The central cylinder is connected to a tubular truss to four cylinders placed around the circumference of the platform. The central cylinder is further divided into three compartments: bottom is for potable water, the middle is for the desalination equipment, and the top is the control chamber. A 22-meter (72-foot) tall tower placed on top of the center cylinder supports the two-bladed turbine.[3] The unit was moved into place offshore by a tugboat in the Aegean Archipelagos. The engineers of the system, which is designed for winds as strong as 200 kilometers per hour (125 mph), successfully faced winds up to 120 kilometers per hour (75 mph). The designers had planned to build a larger floating unit capable of producing up to 1 million liters of freshwater in 2010.[4]

Three primary structures for floating wind turbines have emerged in recent years: semi-submersible platforms, tension leg platforms, and spars.

The semi-submersible platform includes columns interconnected by large braces, with the turbine placed center topside. The structure is anchored to the seabed by using typical mooring systems composed of anchors, cables and chains.

The tension leg platform is somewhat similar to the semi-submersible platform in appearance and operation; however it generally sits deeper in the water and is attached to the seabed by stiff vertical cables or "tendons." Both of these structures have the ability to incorporate existing offshore wind turbines and can be built in sheltered harbors before being towed to site. The tension leg platform requires more installation preparation than the semi-submersibles in terms of additional buoyancy systems and seabed anchor placement. In addition, the tension-leg platforms in shallow waters are so far limited to areas of deepwater free from substantial tidal fluctuations and current.[5] They also pose a structural dynamic challenge to their designers due to the coupling that happens between the mooring, the tower, and the turbine, which have very similar natural frequencies.

The spar is a large, single, near completely submersed cylinder, which has a length almost identical to its topside turbine tower. For installation, the spar requires depths of more than 120 meters (395 feet) for tethering to the seabed, where the semi-submersible and tension leg platforms are suitable in depths starting at 50 meters (164 feet).[6] Delivering power to shore from floating turbines is much the same as other offshore wind farms in that cables will travel along the seabed from the turbines to an offshore substation where an export cable will carry the power to shore.

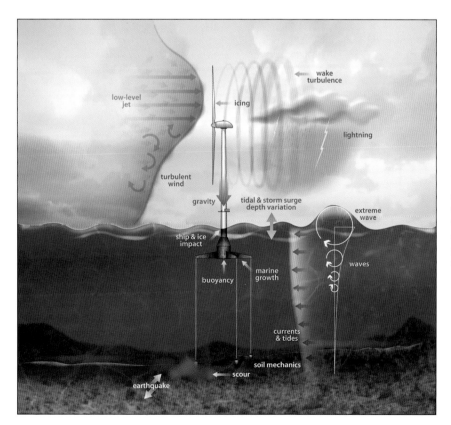

Environmental impacts on floating offshore wind turbines.
Courtesy of the National Renewable Energy Laboratory, Golden, Colorado.

In 2007, Netherlands-based Blue H Technologies became the first company to field a floating turbine for the purpose of testing a utility-grade electric power generation. Blue H's unit, based on the tension leg platform design, was constructed in Brindisi Harbor in Puglia, Italy, and towed to a site 21.3 kilometers (thirteen miles) from shore in water of about 113 meters (370 feet) deep. The platform included an 80-kilowatt turbine outfitted with sensors to record the wave and wind forces experienced. Blue H picked a two-blade turbine instead of a three-blade unit. In a 2008 interview with *M.I.T.'s Technology Review*, Martin Jakubowski, Blue H cofounder and chief technology officer, explained that the two-blade turbine offers thirty to thirty-five revolutions per minute, or double that of three blades, and is also "less susceptible to interference from the back-and-forth swing of the platform under wave action."[7]

The first floating turbine fulfilled its test period and was decommissioned at the end of 2008. Blue H is currently working on a commercial 2.4-megawatt two-blade turbine in Brindisi, which it plans to dispatch to the same site as its test unit in the Adriatic Sea. This will be the first unit of a planned 90-megawatt offshore wind farm, located more than 20 kilometers (thirteen miles) off the Puglia coast.[8]

Blue H has also proposed to build a floating 120-turbine wind farm off the coast of Massachusetts, about twenty-three miles southwest of Martha's Vineyard. A major emphasis for Blue H's turbine development has been on structural weight reduction. The company estimates that its 2.4-megawatt turbine alone will weigh ninety-seven tons, fifty-three tons less than a turbine of comparable output, reducing the turbine's cost and allowing Blue H to deliver wind-generated electricity at seven to eight cents per kilowatt-hour, which is comparable to natural gas and on-shore windpower.[9] Overall, the company believes that a 5-megawatt turbine on its floating platform design should not weigh more than 800 tons.[10]

Blue H's floating wind turbine, based on the tension leg platform design, was built in Brindisi Harbor in Puglia, Italy, and towed to a site about thirteen miles from shore. *Courtesy Blue H Technologies BV, the Netherlands.*

A second floating turbine, with an estimated cost of 75 million euros ($94 million), was deployed by Norwegian energy company Statoil Hydro (now Statoil) in June 2009 for a two-year test at a site about 10 kilometers (six miles) southwest of Karmøy Island. Based on the spar concept developed by Hywind and built by French engineering firm Technip, the platform supports a 2.3-megawatt Siemens turbine with a three-blade rotor diameter of 80 meters (263 feet) on top of a 65-meter (213-foot) high tower. During the installation phase, the platform was towed on its side and upended at the offshore site. Engineers then installed the turbine tower, nacelle and blades with an offshore crane. The unit sits in about 120 meters (395 feet) of water and is attached to the seabed by a three-point mooring system. Nexans produced and laid the power cable to land. The entire test structure weighs about 138 tons and is suitable for water depths of 120 to 700 meters (395 feet to nearly half a mile).[11]

Perhaps the biggest challenge facing all floating wind turbine designers is how to build the most stable platforms without rendering the technology cost prohibitive for commercial use. Turbines for floating structures will be inherently bigger than their counterparts closer to shore — in the range of 5 to 10 megawatts. Numerous additional kilometers of cabling will be required to bring the power to shore. Because of the farther distances from shore, maintenance minimization will be vital to the efficiency and longevity of any deep-sea floating wind farm. While still largely in the experimental stages, floating wind turbine designs will continue to borrow heavily from the engineering successes in the offshore oil and gas industry.

In June 2009, the Norwegian energy company Statoil Hydro (now Statoil) towed its floating wind turbine to an offshore site about six miles southwest of Karmøy Island. *Courtesy of Statoil, Stavanger, Norway.*

Dominique Roddier and Christian Cermelli, naval architects and founders of offshore engineering firm Marine Innovation & Technology, incorporated a floating platform technology that they developed for the oil and gas industry to support giant wind turbines. In partnership with Principle Power, they developed the WindFloat, a semi-submersible platform that includes three closed-loop ballasted columns spaced 35 meters (115 feet) apart and fitted at the base with water entrapment plates. These entrapment plates affixed at the bottom of each column dampen the motion due to the wind and waves, providing continuous stability to the structure.

Another unique aspect of the WindFloat is its asymmetric placement of the turbine on one of the three columns instead of in the middle of the platform. To the untrained eye, it doesn't seem possible that the floating structure could support the size and weight of a plus-5 megawatt turbine in this manner. However, according to Roddier and Cermelli, the WindFloat buoyancy concept secures the turbine in a most stable, upright position. An additional benefit of the WindFloat design is its shallow draft, which allows for quayside construction and towing to the offshore site. This eliminates the need for costly offshore cranes. The WindFloat is secured to the seabed by a conventional mooring system composed of four to six chains or steel cables.[12] "The overall design efficiency and key components in the fabrication, installation, and commissioning of the WindFloat contribute to a system that should be no more expensive than current fixed installation methods for deeper water sites," Roddier wrote in a April 2010 article in *Mechanical Engineering*.[13] Portuguese utility EDP recently partnered with Principle Power to install a full-scale WindFloat prototype off the coast of Portugal by 2011.[14] Principle Power estimates that the WindFloat prototype will cost half as much as Statoil's Hywind prototype.[15]

For eight years, Eystein Borgen, a Norwegian engineer and founder of Sway AS, and his team have designed and tested a floating turbine concept that incorporates a tower extending far below the water's surface. The tower, which is filled with ballast, has its center of gravity located well below the center of buoyancy of the tower, which gives the tower sufficient stability to resist the large loads produced by the nacelle and rotor mounted on top. The floating tower is anchored to the seafloor with a single pipe and a suction anchor. When the wind hits the rotor, the tower tilts about five to eight degrees.

"By tilting the rotor the opposite way which is made possible by placing the rotor downwind of the tower the rotor is kept perfectly aligned with the wind. When the wind changes direction, the entire tower turns around on a sub-sea swivel. This, in turn, makes it possible to reinforce the tower with a tension rod system similar to wire stays on a sailboat mast. Due to the resulting reduction of stresses in the tower, the tower is capable of carrying a much larger turbine, which greatly enhances the total economy," the company said.[16]

In early 2010, Sway began working with Norwegian technology firm Smartmotor on a two-year project to construct a 10-megawatt turbine. Smartmotor's turbine design, which includes a 145-meter (475-feet) rotor diameter, aims to reduce turbine weight and the number of moving parts, as well as promote the use of a gearless generator system. Enova, a Norwegian backer of the project, said the concept would result in higher energy generation for offshore windpower and, thus, lower operating costs.[17]

Ohio-based Nautica Windpower has spent the past several years designing and testing its Asymmetric Floating Tower (AFT), a new type of floating platform that gets stability from the tension of a single mooring line to the seafloor. The company, founded by Larry Viterna and including members of the engineering team for the large horizontal-axis wind turbines initially developed by the U.S. Energy and Interior departments in the early 1980s, proposes a two-blade downwind rotor. It uses a teetered (pivoting) hub, which decouples motion of the rotor plane from the motion of the tower, significantly reducing the damaging loads into the drive train of the wind turbine. Another important design characteristic is that the angle of the tower avoids the possibility of the blades colliding with the tower. Passive wind alignment also eliminates the need for an active yaw system and allows the tower shape to be optimized for thrust load with minimal tower interference that can cause acoustic emissions from the turning blades. The tower of the turbine includes variable buoyancy pumps for stability during installation and lowering of the tower for repair, and a stability arm ensures safe response to rapid changes in wind and high sea states. The AFT would be transported to the offshore site in a horizontal position on a barge. Prior to this step, nearly all the major components of the turbine would be assembled on shore, including the tower, nacelle, rotor hub, one blade, the gearbox and generator. The second blade would be installed at the site using a small crane on the barge. At the offshore site, the tower is lifted upright in the water and the base is secured to the seabed by a single mooring line attached to a simple anchoring system, such as drag-embedded. Viterna expects market entry for Nautica Windpower's 5-megawatt AFT wind turbine to occur by 2013.[18]

Meanwhile, proposed floating turbine designs continue to surface in technical journals and general media reports as the political will and public's interest for wind-generated power strengthens. Sclavounos, of M.I.T., warns that in the early stages of introducing floating units to the market, designers should avoid costly and unproven redesigns of existing wind turbine technology. He advises that current semi-submersible platforms and spurs should carry conventional 5-megawatt turbines, which are already used in shallow-water offshore wind farms.[19] Once floating turbines become established, new designs will inevitably enter the market as designers and offshore wind farm operators seek additional efficiencies and larger electric outputs from their equipment.

Nautica Windpower has designed a floating wind turbine that uses a teetered (pivoting) hub, which decouples motion of the rotor plane from the motion of the tower reducing damaging loads into the drive train of the wind turbine.
Courtesy of Nautica Windpower, Olmsted Falls, Ohio.

A British team of researchers and developers led by OTM Consulting announced in early 2009 the NOVA (Novel Offshore Vertical Axis) project, a 1-gigawatt offshore wind farm of large V-shaped vertical axis turbines. NOVA is based on the so-called "Aerogenerator" concept developed by aeronautical engineer David Sharpe of Wind Power Limited. NOVA's designers claim that unlike traditional, three-blade horizontal axis offshore turbines, the Aerogenerator uses few moving parts and is "insensitive" to changing wind direction. They also note the placement of the generator at the base level allows for the employment of large-scale direct drive units. NOVA plans to develop and install a large-scale demonstrator model offshore within six years, and complete the entire project by 2020.[20] Whether this technology can be successfully deployed on a floating platform remains to be seen.

Even Heronemus' vision of floating multi-rotor turbines, or arrays, may be realized during the next ten to fifteen years. Until his death in 2002, Heronemus, through his firm, Ocean Wind Energy Systems (OWES), formerly located in Amherst, Massachusetts, continued pursuing designs of large-scale arrays. A 1995 study by United Kingdom-based ETSU (now AEA Technology) estimated a 26 percent decrease in system cost for an array of nineteen rotors compared to a single large rotor of comparable swept area and rated power.[21] With conventional turbines pushing size and technology limits, Heronemus noted that arrays of modest size on a single tower may present an attractive alternative to single large rotors, and rotors in an array may be tailored for optimal performance in site-specific wind shear conditions.[22]

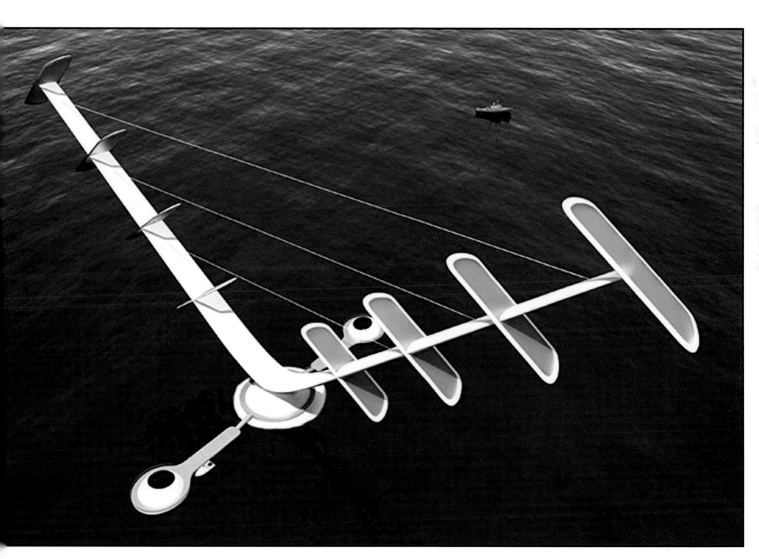

The proposed Aerogenerator, a large V-shaped vertical axis-floating turbine, would generate up to 1-gigawatt of power.
Courtesy of Grimshaw Architects, London, United Kingdom.

OWES's work on the array concept continues under the leadership of Heronemus' daughter Marcia Heronemus-Pate, chief executive officer of the company now based in Tulsa, Oklahoma, and Krishnakant Tekriwal, chief operating officer, in Nagpur, India. In October 2009, the company released its business plan for developing the Gale Force Multi-Rotor Array Turbine System for utility-scale sites. The proposed 6-megawatt array consists of twelve 500-kilowatt banded turbines on a single tower. OWES highlighted a number of advantages of its array over the typical 2-megawatt turbine, including three times higher output using the same swept area and the ability to stop one turbine at a time for maintenance resulting in a loss of only one-twelfth the output.[23] The total weight of the banded airfoil-style turbines in the array is only fifty tons compared to 146 tons for an equivalent 80-meter diameter 2-megawatt size rotor plus nacelle. The proposed design is also seventy percent less expensive and the total weight seventy percent less.[24] Heronemus-Pate said the Gale Force array would first be tested for land use, with the ultimate goal to take it offshore.[25]

Heronemus, the naval architect, designed many floating system variations, and OWES has successfully achieved two patents for some of his designs. Heronemus-Pate is just as convinced as her father was that the full scope of powering much of the world's future energy demands with windpower will be achieved offshore, in deep water where the winds are the most energetic everyday of the year. OWES will be able to use the patented multi-rotor tower with its very lightweight turbines in an offshore setting, the semi-submersible hulls tethered in deep waters with its patented protective, power takeoff buoy to establish offshore wind farms and energy production centers "over the horizon."[26]

The lightweight, component approach will allow for normal and readily available vessels to deploy the wind farms. The full scope of the technology to be tested will increase the power output per tower by at least a factor of three via the ability to optimize each tier to the wind speed and shear of a specific location. The ability to free float on a single tether allows the windship to "find the wind" in its watch circle. Under the OWES plan, offshore deepwater wind farms are to be created where additional energy products will be generated on-site for shipment; products such as fresh water, gaseous hydrogen, liquid hydrogen (as fuel for road transportation and commercial aircraft); anhydrous ammonia for fertilizer and methanol which can be used to produce high octane gasoline that can be sold as a "green" fuel for internal combustion engines. The U.S. wind resource off the coastline, over the horizon, and in the Great Lakes has the potential to generate billions of kilowatt-hours per year of domestic, safe, and pollution-free renewable energy.[27]

Glossary

Sources: Horizon Wind Energy, Houston, Texas,
and Det Norske Veritas, Oslo, Norway.

Air Pollution – Air with contaminants in it that prevent it from dispersing as it normally would and interferes with biological processes.

Alternative Energy – A popular term for "non-conventional" energy like renewables.

Asynchronous Generator – A type of electric generator that produces alternating current (AC) electricity to match an existing power source.

Battery – An energy storage device made up of one or more electrolyte cells. An electrolyte is a non-metallic conductor that carries current.

Breeze – Wind classified as light, gentle, moderate, fresh, or strong.

Carbon Dioxide (CO2) – A colorless, odorless non-combustible gas present in the atmosphere, it is formed by the combustion of carbon and carbon compounds (such as fossil fuels and biomass), by respiration, which is a slow combustion in animals and plants, and by the gradual oxidation of organic matter in the soil. It is also a greenhouse gas that contributes to global climate change.

Carbon Monoxide (CO) – A colorless, odorless but poisonous combustible gas. Carbon monoxide is produced in the incomplete combustion of carbon and carbon compounds, for example, fossil fuels like coal and petroleum.

Central Power Plant – A large power plant that generates power for distribution to multiple customers.

Chemical Energy – The energy liberated in a chemical reaction, as in the combustion of fuels.

Circuit – A device, or system of devices, that allows electrical current to flow through and voltage to occur across positive and negative terminals.

Circuit Breaker – A device used to interrupt or break an electrical circuit when an overload condition exists. Circuit breakers are used to protect electrical equipment from potential damage.

Climate – The prevailing or average weather conditions of a geographic region.

Coating – Metallic, inorganic or organic material applied to steel surfaces for prevention of corrosion.

Conductor – The material through which electricity is transmitted, such as an electrical wire.

Conduit – A tubular material used to encase and protect electrical conductors.

Constant-Speed Wind Turbines – Wind turbines that operate at a constant rpm (rotor revolutions per minute). They're designed for optimal energy capture at a specific rotor diameter and particular wind speed.

Conventional Fuel – Fossil fuels such as coal, oil, and natural gas.

Converter – A device for transforming electricity to a desired quality and quantity.

Cut-In Wind Speed – Lowest mean wind speed at hub height at which a wind turbine produces power.

Cut-Out Wind Speed – Highest mean wind speed at hub height at which a wind turbine is designed to produce power.

Cycle – In alternating current electricity, the current flows in one direction from zero to a maximum voltage, then goes back down to zero, then to a maximum voltage in the opposite direction. This comprises one cycle. The number of complete cycles per second determines the current frequency. In the United States the standard for alternating current is 60 cycles.

Cyclone – Air spinning inward toward centers of low air pressure. Cyclones spin counterclockwise in the Northern Hemisphere and clockwise in the Southern Hemisphere.

Davit Crane – A crane that projects over the side of an installation for moving cargo.

Deregulation – The process of changing policies and laws of regulation in order to increase competition among suppliers of commodities and services. The Energy Policy Act initiated deregulation of the electric power industry in 1992.

Direct Current – A type of electricity transmission and distribution by which electricity flows in one direction through the conductor. Usually the electricity is a relatively low voltage and high current. Direct current is abbreviated as DC.

Distribution – The process of distributing electricity. Distribution usually refers to the portion of power lines between a utility's power pole and transformer and a customer's point of connection.

Doldrums – A narrow, virtually windless zone near the Equator, created as heated air rises upward, leaving the ocean's surface calm and glassy.

Downburst – A severe localized downdraft from a thunderstorm. Also called a microburst.

Downwind Wind Turbine – A horizontal axis wind turbine in which the rotor is downwind of the tower.

Electricity – The energy of moving electrons, the current of which is used as a source of power.

Electricity Generation – The process of producing electricity by transforming other forms or sources of energy into electrical energy. Electricity is measured in kilowatt hours (kWh).

Emission – A substance or pollutant emitted as a result of a process.

Energy – The capacity for work. Energy can be converted into different forms, but the total amount of energy remains the same.

Energy Storage – The process of storing or converting energy from one form to another for later use. An example of a storage device is a battery.

Environment – All the natural and living things around us. The earth, air, weather, plants, and animals all make up our environment.

Fatigue – Degradation of the material caused by cyclic loading.

Foundation – The foundation of a support structure for a wind turbine is a structural or geotechnical component, or both, extending from the seabed downwards.

Frequency – The number of cycles through which an alternating current passes per second, measured in hertz.

Fuel – Material that can be consumed to make energy.

Gearbox – A protective casing for a system of gears.

Generator – A device for converting mechanical energy to electrical energy.

Gigawatt (GW) – A unit of power equal to 1 million kilowatts.

Global Warming – A term used to describe the increase in average global temperatures due to the greenhouse effect.

Green Power – A popular term for energy produced from renewable energy resources.

Greenhouse Effect – The heating effect resulting from long wave radiation from the sun being trapped by greenhouse gases that have been produced from natural and human sources.

Greenhouse Gases – Gases such as water vapor, carbon dioxide, methane, and low-level ozone that are transparent to solar radiation, but opaque to long wave radiation. These gases contribute to the greenhouse effect and, consequently, Global Warming.

Grid (also "Power Grid" and "Utility Grid") – A common term referring to an electricity transmission and distribution system.

Gust – A sudden brief increase in the speed of the wind.

Hertz (Hz) – A measure of the number of cycles or wavelengths of electrical energy per second. The United States electricity supply has a standard frequency of 60 hertz.

Horizontal-Axis Wind Turbines – Turbines on which the axis of the rotor's rotation is parallel to the wind stream and the ground.

Hub Height – Height of center of swept area of wind turbine rotor, measured from mean sea level.

Idling – Condition of a wind turbine, which is rotating slowly and not producing power.

J-Tube – A tube mounted in or at the structure for guiding cable between seabed and installation topsides, its shape resembles the letter "J."

Jet Stream – A meandering and relatively narrow belt of strong winds embedded in the normal wind flow, generally found at high altitudes.

Joule (J) – A metric unit of energy or work; one joule per second equals 1 watt.

Kilowatt (kW) – A standard unit of electrical power equal to 1,000 watts.

Kilowatt-Hour (kWh) – A unit or measure of electricity supply or consumption of 1,000 watts over the period of one hour.

Kinetic Energy – Energy available as a result of motion. (Kinetic energy is equal to one half the mass of the body in motion multiplied by the square of its speed.)

Knot – One nautical mile per hour (1.15 mph).

Leading Edge – The surface part of a wind turbine blade that first comes into contact with the wind.

Lift – The force that pulls a wind turbine blade.

Mean Power Output (of a Wind Turbine) – The average power output of a wind energy conversion system at any given mean wind speed.

Mean Wind Speed – The average wind speed over a specified time period and height above the ground.

Mechanical Energy – The energy possessed by an object due to its motion (kinetic energy) or its potential energy.

Median Wind Speed – The wind speed with fifty percent probability of occurring.

Megawatt (MW) – The standard measure of electric power plant generating capacity. One megawatt is equal to 1,000 kilowatts or 1 million watts.

Megawatt-hour (MWh) – 1,000 kilowatt-hours or 1 million watt-hours.

Met Tower – Meteorological towers erected to verify the wind resource found within a certain area.

Nitrogen Oxides (NOx) – The products of all combustion processes formed by the combination of nitrogen and oxygen. Nitrogen oxides and sulfur dioxide are the two primary causes of acid rain.

Non-Renewable Fuels – Fuels that cannot be easily renewed or reproduced, such as oil, natural gas, and coal.

Offshore Wind Turbine Structure – A structural system consisting of a support structure for an offshore wind turbine and a foundation for the support structure.

Offshore Substation – A collective term for high voltage AC (transformer) and high voltage DC (converter) platforms as well as associated accommodation platforms located offshore.

Peak Wind Speed – The maximum instantaneous wind speed that occurs within a specific period of time.

Power – Energy that is available for doing work.

Power Grid (also "Utility Grid") – A common term referring to an electricity transmission and distribution system.

Power Quality – Stability of frequency and voltage and lack of electrical noise on the power grid.

Prevailing Wind Direction – The direction from which the wind predominantly blows as a result of the seasons, high and low pressure zones, the tilt of the earth on its axis, and the rotation of the earth.

Rated Power – Quality of power assigned, generally by a manufacturer, for a specified operating condition of a component, device or equipment. For a wind turbine, the rated power is the maximum continuous electrical power output which a wind turbine is designed to achieve under normal operating conditions.

Rated Wind Speed – Minimum wind speed at hub height at which a wind turbine's rated power is achieved in the case of a steady wind without turbulence.

Renewable Energy – Derived from resources that are regenerative or that cannot be depleted, types of renewable energy resources include wind, solar, biomass, geothermal, and moving water.

Restructuring – The process of changing the structure of the electric power industry from one of a guaranteed monopoly that is regulated to one of open competition between power suppliers.

Rotor-Nacelle Assembly – Part of the wind turbine carried by the support structure.

Scour Zone – The external region of the wind turbine which is located at the seabed and which is exposed to scour.

Solar Energy – Electromagnetic energy transmitted from the sun (solar radiation).

Splash Zone – The external region of the wind turbine which is most frequently exposed to wave action.

Standstill – The condition of a wind turbine generator system that is stopped.

Step-Up Gearbox – A step-up gearbox increases turbine electricity production in stages by increasing the number of generator revolutions produced by the rotor revolutions.

Submerged Zone – The part of the wind turbine installation which is below the splash zone, including buried parts.

Sulfur Dioxide (SO2) – A colorless gas released as a by-product of combusted fossil fuels containing sulfur. The two primary sources of acid rain are sulfur dioxide and nitrogen oxides.

Sustainable Energy – Energy that takes into account present needs while not compromising the availability of energy or a healthy environment in the future.

Tide – Regular and predictable movements of the sea generated by astronomical forces.

Tower – Structural component, which forms a part of the support structure for a wind turbine, usually extending from somewhere above the still water level to just below the nacelle of the wind turbine.

Trade Wind – The consistent system of prevailing winds occupying most of the tropics. They constitute the major component of the general circulation of the atmosphere. Trade winds blow northeasterly in the Northern Hemisphere and southeasterly in the Southern Hemisphere. The trades, as they are sometimes called, are the most persistent wind system on earth.

Turbine – Also see "Wind Turbine." A term used for a wind energy conversion device that produces electricity.

Turbulence – A swirling motion of the atmosphere that interrupts the flow of wind.

Unidirectional – Wind and/or waves acting in one single direction.

Utility Areas – Areas for power generation, power conversion, switchboards, workshops, storage areas and general machinery.

Utility Grid – Also see "Power Grid." A common term referring to an electricity transmission and distribution system.

Variable-Speed Wind Turbines – Turbines in which the rotor speed increases and decreases with changing wind speeds. Sophisticated power control systems are required on variable speed turbines to insure that their power maintains a constant frequency compatible with the grid.

Volt – A unit of electrical force.

Voltage – The amount of electromotive force, measured in volts, that exists between two points.

Watt (W) – The rate of energy transfer (from an outlet to an appliance, for example). Wattage is calculated by multiplying voltage by current.

Watt-Hour (Wh) – A unit of electricity consumption of one watt over the period of one hour.

Wind – Moving air. The wind's movement is caused by the sun's heat, the earth, and the oceans, forcing air to rise and fall in cycles.

Wind Energy – (Also see "Wind Power") Power generated by converting the mechanical energy of the wind into electrical energy through the use of a wind generator.

Wind Energy Conversion System (WECS) – An apparatus for converting wind energy to mechanical energy, making it available for powering machinery and operating electrical generators.

Wind Generator – A wind energy conversion system designed to produce electricity.

Wind Power – Also see "Wind Energy." Power generated by converting the mechanical energy of the wind into electrical energy through the use of a wind generator.

Wind Power Plant – A group of wind turbines interconnected to a common utility system.

Wind Resource Assessment – The process of characterizing the wind resource and its energy potential for a specific site or geographical area.

Wind Rose – A diagram that indicates the average percentage of time that the wind blows from different directions, on a monthly or annual basis.

Wind Shear – Variation of wind speed across a plane perpendicular to the wind direction.

Wind Speed – The rate of flow of wind when it blows undisturbed by obstacles.

Wind Speed Frequency Curve – A curve that indicates the number of hours per year that specific wind speeds occur.

Wind Speed Profile – A profile of how the wind speed changes at different heights above the surface of the ground or water.

Wind Turbine – A term used for a wind energy conversion device that produces electricity.

Wind Turbine Rated Capacity – The amount of power a wind turbine can produce at its rated wind speed.

Wind Velocity – The wind speed and direction in an undisturbed flow.

Windmill – A wind energy conversion system that is used to grind grain. However, the word windmill is commonly used to refer to all types of wind energy conversion systems.

Windpower Profile – The change in the power available in the wind due to changes in the wind speed or velocity.

Yawing – Rotation of the rotor axis of a wind turbine about a vertical axis.

Appendix

Industry Associations

Global Wind Energy Council
Renewable Energy House
Rue d'Arlon 63-65
1040 Brussels
Belgium
Tel: +32-2-400-1029
Fax: +32-2-546-1944
Website: www.gwec.net

North America

American Wind Energy Association
1501 M Street NW
Suite 1000
Washington, D.C. 20005
U.S.A.
Tel: +202-383-2500
Fax: +202-383-2505
Website: www.awea.org

Asociación Mexicana de Energía Eólica
Ave. Jaime Balmes No. 11 L 130 F
Col. Los Morales Chapultepec México,
D.F. 11510
Mexico
Tel: +52-55-5395-9559
Website: www.amdee.org

Canadian Wind Energy Association
Suite 810
170 Laurier Avenue West
Ottawa, Ontario
Canada K1P 5V5
Tel: +613-234-8716
Fax: +613-234-5642
Website: www.canwea.org

Great Lakes Renewable Energy Association
Website: www.glrea.org

Great Lakes Wind Cooperative
c/o Great Lakes Commission
Eisenhower Corporate Park
2805 S. Industrial Hwy, Suite 100
Ann Arbor, Michigan 48104
U.S.A.
Tel: +734-971-9135
Fax: +734-971-9150
Website: www.glrea.org

Marine Technology Society
5565 Sterrett Place, Suite 108
Columbia, Maryland 21044
U.S.A.
Tel: +410-884-5330
Website: www.mtsociety.org

Windustry
(Great Lakes Regional Wind Energy Institute)
2105 1st Avenue South
Minneapolis Minnesota 55404
U.S.A.
Tel: +612-870-3461
Fax: +612-813-5612
Website: www.windustry.org

Europe

European Wind Energy Association
Renewable Energy House
Rue d'Arlon 63-65
1040 Brussels
Belgium
Tel: +32-2-546-1940
Website: www.ewea.org

Asociación Empresarial Eólica
Serrano, 143
28006 Madrid
Spain
Tel: +34 917 451 276
Fax: +34 917 451 277
Website: www.aeeolica.es

Associacao de Energias Renovaveis
Av. Sidónio Pais n°18 r/c Esq.
1050-215 Lisbon
Portugal
Tel: +351-213-151-621
Fax: +351-213-151-622
Website: www.apren.pt

Associazione Nazionale Energia del Vento
Via Palestro, 1
00185 Rome
Italy
Tel: +39-06-4201-4701
Fax: +39-06-4200-4838
Website: www.anev.org

Baltic Wind Energy Association
Barnstorfer Weg 26
18057 Rostock
Germany
Tel: +381-375-65-929
Website: www.rotorwerk.de

British Wind Energy Association
RenewableUK
Greencoat House
Francis Street
London, SW1P 1DH
United Kingdom
Tel: +44-(0)20-7901-3000
Fax: +44-(0)20-7901-3001
Website: www.bwea.com

Bundesverband WindEnergie e.V.
Marienstrasse 19-20
10117 Berlin
Germany
Tel: +49-30-28-48-21-06
Fax: +49-30-28-48-21-07
Website: www.wind-energie.de

Eesti Tuuleenergia Assotsiatsioon
Regati pst. 1
11911 Tallinn
Estonia
Tel: +372-6-396-610
Fax: +372-6-396-620
Website: www.tuuleenergia.ee

Fédération de l'Energie d'Origine Renouvelable et Alternative (EDORA)
Rue Royale 35
1000 Brussels
Belgium
Tel: +32-2-217-9682
Fax: +32-2-223-5984
Website: www.edora.be

Finnish Wind Power Association
Itsenäisyydenkatu 2
33100 Tampere
Finland
Tel: +358-40-771-6114
Website: www.tuulivoimayhdistys.fi

France Energie Eolienne/Syndicat des énergies renouvelables
13-15 rue de la Baume
75008 Paris
France
Tel: +33-1-48-78-05-60
Fax: +33-1-48-78-09-07
Website: www.fee.asso.fr

Irish Wind Energy Association
Sycamore House
Millennium Park
Osberstown, Naas, Co. Kildare
Ireland
Tel: +353-45-899341
Fax: +353-45-854958
Website: www.iwea.com

Latvian Association of Wind Energy
Akadmijas laukums 1
Riga, LV-1050
Latvia
Tel: +371-29-411-216
Website: www.windenergy.lv

Lithuanian Wind Power Association
K. Donelaičio g. 62 -315
44248 Kaunas
Lithuania
Tel: +370-37-211-303
Fax: +370-37-211-303
Website: www.lvea.lt

Nederlandse Wind Energie Associatie
Korte Elisabethstraat 6
3511 JG Utrecht
The Netherlands
Tel: +31-30-231-6977
Website: www.nwea.nl

Offshore Center Denmark
Niels Bohrs Vej 6
6700 Esbjerg
Denmark
Tel: +45-3697-3670
Fax: +45-3697-36-79
Website: www.offshorecenter.dk

OWEMES Association
Via Antonio Serra 62
00191 Rome
Italy
Tel: +39-06-4542-6060
Website: www.owemes.org

Polish Wind Energy Association
al. Wojska Polskiego 154
71-324 Szczecin
Poland
Tel: +48-91-486-2530
Fax: +48-91-486-2538
Website: www.pwea.pl

Svensk Vindenergi
Olof Palmes gata 31
101 53 Stockholm
Sweden
Tel: +46 8-677-25-00
Fax: +46 8-677-25-06
Website: www.svenskvindenergi.org

Asia

Chinese Wind Energy Association
11th Floor
Yiheng Mansion, No. 28
North Third Ring Road East
Chaoyang
Beijing, 100013
China
Tel: +86-10-0505-2227
Website: www.cwea.org.cn

Clean Energy Council
Suite 201
18 Kavanagh Street
Southbank VIC 3006
Australia
Tel: +61-3-9929-4100
Fax: +61-3-9929-4101
Website: www.cleanenergycouncil.org

Indian Wind Energy Association
PHD House, 3rd Floor
Opp. Asian Games Village
August Kranti Marg,
New Delhi 110016
India
Tel: +91-11-2652-3042
Website: www.inwea.org

Japanese Wind Energy Association
Kita no Maru Koen 2-1
Chiyoda-ku, Tokyo 102-0091
Japan
Tel: +81-298-58-7275
Website: http://ppd.jsf.or.jp/jwea

Japanese Wind Power Association
Bi-O-Re Akiabara Bldg. 10
Kanda Matsunaga-Cho 18-1
Chiyoda-ku Tokyo 101-0023
Japan
Tel: +81-3-5297-5578
Website: www.jwpa.jp

New Zealand Wind Energy Association
Level 7, St John House
114 The Terrace
Wellington 6011
New Zealand
Tel: +64-4-499-5046
Fax: +64 4 473 6754
Website: www.windenergy.org.nz

Small Offshore Turbine Providers

Ampair
Park Farm
West End Lane
Warfield
Berkshire
RG42 5RH
United Kingdom
Tel: +44-1344-303-313
Website: www.ampair.com

Eclectic Energy Limited (DuoGen)
Unit 22, Sherwood Networkcentre
Sherwood Energy Village
Ollerton
Nottinghamshire
NG22 9PR
United Kingdom
Tel: +44 1623-835-400
Website: www.eclectic-energy.co.uk
or www.duogen.co.uk

ITT Corporation (AeroGen)
Bingley Road
Hoddesdon
Hertfordshire
EN11 0BU
United Kingdom
Tel: +44-1992-450-145
Website: www.itt.com

Kiss Energy Systems
Private Bag 195
Carenage Post Office
Trinidad, West Indies
Tel: +868-634-4929
Website: www.kissenergy.com

Marlec Engineering Co. Ltd.
(Rutland Windchargers)
Rutland House
Trevithick Road
Corby Northants
NN17 5XY
United Kingdom
Tel: +44-1536-201-588
Website: www.marlec.co.uk

**Southwest Windpower
(Air Breeze and Air-X)**
1801 W. Route 66
Flagstaff, Arizona 86001
U.S.A.
Tel: +928-779-9463
Website: www.windenergy.com

Windbugger
2543 Gulfstream Lane
Ft. Lauderdale, FL 33312
U.S.A.
Tel: +954-684-3528
Website: www.windbugger.com

U.S. Government Sources

Energy Information Administration
U.S. Department of Energy
1000 Independence Avenue SW
Washington, D.C. 20585
U.S.A.
Tel: +202-586-8800
Website: www.eia.doe.gov

National Renewable Energy Laboratory
U.S. Department of Energy
1617 Cole Boulevard
Golden, Colorado 80401

U.S.A.
Tel: +303-275-3000
Website: www.nrel.gov

Wind & Hydropower Technologies Program
Energy Efficiency and Renewable Energy
U.S. Department of Energy
1000 Independence Avenue SW
Washington, D.C. 20585
U.S.A.
Tel: +202-586-9220
Website: www.eere.energy.gov

Offshore Wind Information Sources

4C Offshore
Website: www.4coffshore.com
The company's Wind Farms Database contains details on more than 600 wind farms in over thirty countries.

OCS Alternative Energy and Alternate Use Programmatic EIS Information Center
Website: www.ocsenergy.anl.gov
The website is the online center for public information and involvement in the U.S. Outer Continental Shelf Alternative Energy and Alternate Use Programmatic Environmental Impact Statement.

Offshore-Wind
Website: www.offshore-wind.de
The website, developed by the German Energy Agency – Energy Systems and Systems Services, offers insights into the developments of Germany's offshore wind farms.

OffshoreWind.net
Website: www.offshorewind.net
The website, which was started by a university student with an interest in offshore wind energy in the United States and Canada, aims to build a resource of factual information without bias or agenda for the purpose of education.

**Offshore Windfarms:
Putting Energy into the UK**
Website: www.offshorewindfarms.co.uk
The website developed by COWRIE – Collaborative Offshore Wind Research Into The Environment – offers a wealth of information about the United Kingdom's offshore wind developments.

The Wind Power
Web: www.thewindpower.net
The website serves as a database on wind turbine manufacturers and wind farms.

Publications

North American Windpower
100 Willenbrock Road
Oxford, Connecticut 06478
U.S.A.
Tel: +203-262-4670
Fax: +203-262-4680
Website: www.nawindpower.com

Offshore Wind Magazine
Westerlaan 1
3016 CK Rotterdam
The Netherlands
Tel: +31-10-209-2600
Fax: +31-10-436-8134
Website: www.offshorewind.biz

Offshore Wind Wire
Website: http://offshorewindwire.com

Renewable Energy World
PennWell International Publications Limited
Warlies Park House
Horseshoe Hill, Upshire
Essex
EN9 3SR
United Kingdom
Tel: +44-1992-656-600
Website: www.renewableenergyworld.com

Sun & Wind Energy
BVA Bielefelder Verlag
Niederwall 53
33602 Bielefeld
Germany
Tel: +49-521-595-538
Website: www.sunwindenergy.com

Wind Energy News
P.O. Box 876
Putney, Vermont
U.S.A.
Website: www.windenergynews.com

Wind Energy Update
7-9 Fashion Street
London
E1 6PX
United Kingdom
Tel: +44-207-375-7500
Website: www.windenergyupdate.com

Wind Engineering
Multi-Science Publishing Co. Ltd
5 Wates Way
Brentwood

Essex
CM15 9TB
United Kingdom
Tel: +44-1277-224-632
Website: www.multi-science.co.uk/windeng.htm

Wind Systems Magazine
266D Yeager Parkway
Pelham, Alabama 35124
U.S.A.
Tel: +800-366-2185
Fax: +205-380-1580
Website: www.windsystemsmag.com

Wind Today
3065 Pershing Court
Decatur, Illinois 62526
U.S.A.
Tel: +800-728-7511
Fax: +217-877-6647
Website: www.windtoday.net

Wind-Works
606 Hillcrest Dr.
Bakersfield, California 93305
U.S.A.
Tel: + 661-325-9590
Website: www.wind-works.org
The website, developed by 35-year industry veteran, writer, and lecturer Paul Gipe, is an online archive of articles and commentary primarily on wind energy, feed-in tariffs, and advanced renewable tariffs.

Windpower Monthly
P.O. Box 1623
8250 Egaa
Denmark
Tel: +45-8636-5900
Fax: +45-8622-1850
Website: www.windpowermonthly.com

WindStats Newsletter
P.O. Box 1623
8250 Egaa
Denmark
Tel: +45-8636-5900
Fax: +45-8622-1850
Website: www.windstats.com

Windtech International
Dr C Hofstede de Grootkade 28
9718 KB Groningen
The Netherlands
Tel: +31-50-579-8924
Fax: +31-50-579-8925
Website: www.windtech-international.com

Windmill History
Associations and Publications

The International Molinological Society
(Publication: International Molinology)
Tony Bonson, Editor
14 Falmouth Road
Congleton
CW12 3BH
United Kingdom
Tel: +44-1260-276-351
Website: www.timsmills.info

**The International Molinological Society
of America**
(Publication: The Mill Monitor)
Ben Smith, Editor
16 Mountain Ave.
Somerville, New Jersey 08876
U.S.A.

Society for the Preservation of Old Mills
Publication: Old Mill News
Sandra Jones Birkland, Editor
122 Calistoga Road #134
Santa Rosa, California 95409
Tel: +707-477-6305
Website: www.spoom.org

William Heronemus – Windpower Pioneer
Website: www.theheronemusproject.com
*This website was developed as a comprehensive
collection of photos, images, papers, and articles chronicling
Heronemus' work in the wind energy field.*

Winds of Change
Website: www.windsofchange.dk
*Developed by early blade manufacturer Erik Grove-
Nielsen, the website tells the story of windpower in photos
from the years 1975-2000. You can download PDF copies
of early brochures from eighty-four wind turbine companies,
as well as high resolution images of many turbines.*

Windmillers' Gazette
T. Lindsay Baker, Editor
P.O. Box 507
Rio Vista, Texas 76093
Website: www.windmillersgazette.com

Windmill Study Unit
American Topical Association
(Publication: Windmill Whispers)
Fred Atkins, Editor
35 Laxton Way
Sittingbourne
Kent
ME10 2QL
United Kingdom
Website: www.wsuweb.eu

End Notes

Chapter 1

1. Hans E. Wulff. *The Traditional Crafts of Persia: Their Development, Technology, and Influence on Eastern and Western Civilization.* Cambridge, Massachusetts: The M.I.T. Press, 1966; 284-285.

2. Frans Bouwers, editor of *Levende Molens*, Ekeren, Belgium; e-mail interview, March 31, 2010.

3. Ibid.

4. Stefanos Nomikos, author of *The Windmills of the Cyclades* (Athens, Greece: Greek Molinolojicel Society, 1993), and former president of the Greek Molinological Society; e-mail interview with author, February 8, 2010.

5. George Speis, Greek windmill historian, Athens, Greece; e-mail interview with author, February 8, 2010.

6. Michael Haverson. "Greek Windmill Sails: Pictorial evidence for the adoption of jib sails." (Paper presented at the 12th annual meeting of The International Molinological Society, 2007).

7. Nomikos, interview.

8. Chris Gibbings. "Small Composite Windmills on the Coasts of Europe," *International Molinology*, December 2001; 2-6.

9. Charles A. Coleman Jr. and William Marks. *The History of Windpower on Martha's Vineyard.* The National Association of Wind-Power Resources, Inc., 1981; 7-10.

10. Ibid, 11.

11. Ibid, 15.

12. Brouwers, interview.

13. Brouwers, interview.

14. Walter Minchinton. "Wind Power," *History Today*, March 1980; 35-36.

15. T. Lindsay Baker. "Bilge Pumping By Wind Power," *Windmillers' Gazette*, Winter 1990; 9.

16. Ibid.

17. "Windmills on sailing ships: Work the pumps while the men sleep," *Popular Mechanics*, October 1906; 1026.

18. Etienne Rogier. "The Polar Wind Machines: The wind generator on the Fram during Nansen's 1893-96 Arctic expedition," *Windmillers' Gazette*, Spring 1998; 7-11.

19. Catalogue 19th Edition Ontario Wind Engine & Pump Co., Toronto, Canada (1902): 25 (from the research files of T. Lindsay Baker, editor, *Windmillers' Gazette*).

20. Fred Atkins. "Windmill on Scott's 'Discovery'," *International Molinology*, December 2009; 36.

21. T. Lindsay Baker and Etienne Rogier. "'The Wireless Means Life Itself': The Wind Generator and Radio on the 1937 Russian North Pole Expedition," *Windmillers' Gazette*, Winter 2002; 6.

22. Ibid, 8.

Chapter 2

1. "The Sources of Energy in Nature," *Mechanical Engineering*, 1881; 321.

2. "Mr. Brush's Windmill Dynamo," *Scientific American*, December 20, 1890; 389.

3. George Wise, editor. "Brush, Charles Francis," *American National Biography Online*, http://www.amb.org/articles/13/13-00214.html (accessed January 12, 2007).

4. "Mr. Brush's Windmill Dynamo," 389.

5. Povl-Otto Nissen, chairman, The Poul la Cour Museum's Friends. "A visit to the Poul la Cour Museum," http://www.povlonis.dk/Plc/visiteng.html (accessed June 5, 2007).

6. "Introduction to Energy Storage," University of Colorado at Boulder, http://www.colorado.edu/engineering/energystorage/intro.html (accessed June 14, 2010).

7. "Commercial utilization of solar radiation and wind power," *Scientific American*, January 21, 1911; 65.

8. Anton Flettner. *The Story of the Rotor (Mein Weg zum Rotor)*. New York, New York: F. O. Willhofft, 1926; 88.

9. Ibid, 99.

10. Ibid, 104-106.

11. Willy Ley. "What Future for Wind Power?" *Science Digest*, August 1954; 84-85.

12. W. E. Warrilow. "Electricity from the Wind: Mighty Cloud-High Dynamos to Harness Natural Forces," *Modern Wonder*, September 3, 1938; 3.

13. Heiner Dörner. "Windenergy History." http://www.heiner-doener-windenergie.de; e-mail interview, December 16, 2009.

14. Biographic notes of Hermann Honnef, http://www.munzinger.de/search/portrait/Hermann+Honnef/0/5072.html (translated by Dietmar Jost, Düsseldorf, Germany) e-mail February 9, 2010.

15. "Big Windmill," *Fortune*, November 1941; 85.

16. F. A. Annett. "World's Largest Wind-Turbine Plant Nears Completion," *Power*, June 1941; 59.

17. "Watts from Wind," *Business Week*, November 24, 1945; 50.

18. D. Stein, Memorandum No. 4: "Wind power stations in Denmark: Use of wind power in the Eastern territories," Working Group of the Reich "Wind Power" (April 23, 1942) (translated by Dietmar Jost, Düsseldorf, Germany).

19. Paul N. Vosburgh. *Commercial Applications of Wind Power*. New York, New York: Van Nostrand Reinhold Company, 1983; 29.

20. Stein, 1942.

21. Ibid.

22. Percy H. Thomas, Office of the Chief Engineer, Federal Power Commission, "The Wind Power Aerogenerator Twin-Wheel Type: A Study," March 1946; 5.

23. David Rittenhouse Inglis. *Wind Power and Other Energy Options*. Ann Arbor, Michigan: The University of Michigan Press, 1978; 8.

24. Christopher Gillis. *Windpower*. Atglen, Pennsylvania: Schiffer Publishing Ltd., 2008; 58.

25. NASA Lewis Research Center, Cleveland, Ohio. "Wind Energy Systems: A Non-Pollutive, Non-Depletable Energy," December 1973.

26. Ron Chernow. "Heronemus the Wind King," *Quest*, January/February 1978; 13.

27. Ibid, 14.

28. Marcia Heronemus-Pate, president, OWES, LLC, Tulsa, Oklahoma, telephone interview, December 10, 2009.

29. William E. Heronemus. "Pollution-Free Energy from the Offshore Winds," 1 (paper presented at the 8th Annual Conference and Exposition, Marine Technology Society, Washington, D.C., September 11-13, 1972).

30. Ibid, 2-3.

31. Chernow, 20.

32. Heronemus, 2.

33. Ibid, 20.

34. Chernow, 14.

35. David Rittenhouse Inglis. "Power from the Ocean Winds," *Environment*, October 1978; 18.

36. Woody Stoddard. "Appreciation: The Life and Work of Bill Heronemus, wind engineering pioneer," *Wind Engineering*, 2002; 337.

37. Inglis, 18.

38. Ibid, 19.

39. David A. Spera, Bibliography of NASA-Related Publications on Wind Turbine Technology, 1973-1995 (DOE/NASA/5776-3 or NASA CR-195462) (April 1995), 5.

40. Ibid, 15.

41. J. F. Manwell, J.G. McGowan, and F.S. Stoddard. "The UMass Wind Turbine WF-1, A Retrospective." University of Massachusetts Amherst, Center for Energy Efficiency & Renewable Energy, http://www.ceere.org/rerl/WF1/ (accessed April 15, 2010).

42. Ibid.

43. OWES, LLC, Tulsa, Oklahoma. "Company History and Bios." http://www.oceanwindenergysystems.com (accessed November 8, 2009).

Chapter 3

1. Christopher N. Elkinton, James E. Manwell, and Jon G. McGowan, University of Massachusetts Amherst. "Optimizing the Layout of Offshore Wind Energy Systems," *Marine Technology Society Journal*, Summer 2008; 19.

2. Peter Musgrove. *Wind Power*. Cambridge, United Kingdom: Cambridge University Press, 2010; 138-140.

3. P. L. Surman and D. J. Milborrow, Central Electricity Generating Board, London. "The CEGB wind energy programme – 10 years back and 10 years forward." (Wind Energy Conversion 1988, by Mechanical Engineering Publications Ltd.), paper for the Proceedings of the 10th British Wind Energy Association Wind Energy Conference), 9.

4. Peter Musgrove, wind energy engineer and author; e-mail interview, May 4, 2010.

5. Staffan Engström, managing director, Ägir konsult AB, Lidingö, Sweden; e-mail interview, February 14, 2010.

6. Ibid.

7. Ibid.

8. Peter Christiansen, project manager, SEAS-NVE Holding A/S, Haslev, Denmark; e-mail interview, April 9, 2010.

9. Ibid.

10. Ibid.

11. Mike Flood. "Danish wind farms head out to sea." *New Scientist*, October 20, 1990; 26.

12. Christiansen, interview.

13. Ibid.

14. Ibid.

15. Danish Wind Industry Association Website, http://www.windpower.org/en/pictures/offshore.htm (accessed July 23, 2007).

16. Christopher Gillis. *Windpower*. Atglen, Pennsylvania: Schiffer Publishing Ltd., 2008; 78.

17. Ibid.

18. David Scott. "Harnessing sea breezes," *Popular Science*, March 1991; 24.

19. Engström, interview.

20. Gaetano Gaudiosi. "Offshore wind energy prospects," *Renewable Energy*, January 1999; 832-833.

21. Gillis, 78.

Chapter 4

1. Brian Braginton-Smith, The Conservation Consortium, South Yarmouth, Massachusetts, "Commentary: Offshore Wind Energy, Frontier Outposts for Sustainable Seas," *Marine Technology Society Journal*, Winter 2002: 11.

2. "Horns Rev reveals the real hazardous of offshore wind," *Modern Power Systems*, October 2004: 27-29.

3. Simon-Philippe Breton and Geir Moe, "Status, plans and technologies for offshore wind turbines in Europe and North America," *Renewable Energy*, 2009: 648.

4. "Reaping the Whirlwind? Europe's Big Wind Subsidy Race," *The New York Times*, February 24, 2010.

5. "Offshore wind farm opens off the coast of the Netherlands," *The New York Times*, April 18, 2007.

6. Royal Dutch Shell, "The Netherlands' first wind farm in the North Sea is performing well," April 4, 2007.

7. Dirk Berkhout, Econcern, the Netherlands, "A wind power landmark on the horizon," *Modern Power Systems*, September 2008: 43.

8. Brian Snyder and Mark J. Kaiser, "Offshore wind power in the U.S.: Regulatory issues and models for negotiation," *Energy Policy*, 2009: 4445.

9. "300-MW of Offshore Wind Planned in Netherlands," *RenewableEnergyWorld.com*, January 29, 2009.

10. Management Unit of the North Sea Mathematical Models, a department of the Royal Belgian Institute of Natural Sciences, http://www.mumm.ac.be/EN/Management/Sea-based/windmills.php (accessed May 31, 2010).

11. Frank Coenen, chief executive officer, Belwind nv. E-mail interview, December 11, 2009.

12. Management Unit of the North Sea Mathematical Models, a department of the Royal Belgian Institute of Natural Sciences.

13. Coenen, interview.

14. "Swedish offshore wind farm gets inaugurated," *Offshore Wind*, May 24, 2010.

15. Staffan Engström, managing director, Ägir konsult AB, Lidingö, Sweden. E-mail interview, June 1, 2010.

16. Sweden 2008, Global Wind Energy Council Web site, http://www.gwec.net (accessed June 13, 2010).

17. Anders Bjartnes, "Norway's first offshore wind farm is given final consent," Rechargenews.com, September 10, 2009.

18. Offshore Statistics January 2009, European Wind Energy Association Web site, http://www.ewea.org (accessed June 13, 2010).

19. Gerard O'Dwyer, "Planning for Finland's largest offshore wind farm is almost," *Windpower Monthly*, January 15, 2010.

20. Offshore Statistics January 2009, European Wind Energy Association.

21. Vytautas Gaizauskas, "Kicking the gas habit: Offshore wind farm for the Baltic states," *Wind Energy Update*, June 11, 2010.

22. British Wind Energy Association, Briefing Sheet: Offshore Wind, September 2005.

23. Tom Meghie, "Crown Estate grabs £5bn for wind farms," *MailOnline*, December 26, 2009.

24. British Wind Energy Association, Briefing Sheet: Offshore Wind.

25. "World's first wind and gas offshore energy project given green light," *PRNewswire-GNN*, February 8, 2007.

26. British Wind Energy Association, Briefing Sheet: Offshore Wind.

27. Chris Rose, "World's first 1GW offshore wind farm," *Wind Directions* (September 2009): 23-24.

28. British Wind Energy Association, "'We can build new UK industry from offshore wind revolution,' says BWEA," January 8, 2010.

29. Tony James, "Turbulent Times," *Engineering & Technology* (July 5-18, 2008): 58.

30. Arklow Offshore Wind Park Web site, http://www.ceoe.udel.edu/windpower/docs/arklow_infosheet_final.pdf (accessed June 3, 2010).

31. National Offshore Wind Association of Ireland, "Announcement Unlocks the Potential of Renewable Energy in Ireland," 2008.

32. Tim O'Brien, "Commitment to wind energy stressed," Irishtimes.com, October 12, 2009.

33. Brian Snyder and Mark J. Kaiser, "A comparison of offshore wind power development in Europe and the U.S.: Patterns and drivers of development," *Applied Energy* (2009): 1845.

34. *European Wind Energy Association, Wind in power: 2009 European statistics* (February 2010), 4.

35. Christopher Gillis, *Windpower* (Atglen Pennsylvania: Schiffer Publishing Ltd., 2008), 59.

36. Sonia Phalnikar, "Germany Charts New Waters with Offshore Wind Energy Plans," *dw-world.de*, July 14, 2008.

37. "Alpha ventus test field: Germany's first offshore wind park," *Offshore-wind.de* (accessed June 4, 2010).

38. "Clipper Windpower Announces Ground Breaking For Offshore Wind Blade Factory," *North American Windpower*, February 19, 2010.

39. *European Wind Energy Association, Oceans of Opportunity: Harnessing Europe's largest domestic energy resource* (September 2009), 58.

40. "English ports in front line of wind farm expansion," *Lloyd's List*, February 14, 2008.

41. Eize de Vries, "Boomtown Bremerhaven: The Offshore Wind Industry Success Story," *Renewable Energy World Magazine*, March 13, 2009.

42. *European Wind Energy Association, Oceans of Opportunity: Harnessing Europe's largest domestic energy resource*, 61.

43. Eddie O'Connor, chief executive officer and founder of Airtricity, Dublin, Ireland, "The European Offshore Supergrid," *Windtech International*, January/February 2007: 8-9.

44. "Offshore wind as Europe's largest untapped energy source," *Construction & Maintenance News* (accessed December 12, 2009).

45. *European Wind Energy Association, Oceans of Opportunity: Harnessing Europe's largest domestic energy resource*, 27.

46. *European Wind Energy Association, Oceans of Opportunity: Harnessing Europe's largest domestic energy resource*, 12-13.

47. Ibid, 14.

48. Ibid, 12.

Chapter 5

1. D.J. De Renzo, editor, Wind Power: Recent Developments (Energy Technology Review, 46) (Park Ridge, New Jersey: Noyes Data Corp., 1979), 53.

2. Bruce H. Bailey and Jeffrey M. Freedman, "A regional assessment of the U.S. offshore wind energy resource through the use of mesoscale modeling," *Marine Technology Society Journal*, Summer 2008: 8.

3. Ibid, 14.

4. Mark Rodgers and Craig Olmsted, Cape Wind Associates, "Engineering and regulatory challenges facing the development of commercially viable offshore wind projects," *Marine Technology Society Journal*, Summer 2008: 44-45.

5. Willow Outhwaite and Sarah Taijel, HC Offshore Ltd., "Offshore Wind – Worth the Risk?" *Windtech International*, November/December 2009: 25.

6. Michael W. Drunsic, technical analyst, GEC, a DNV company, Lowell, Massachusetts, "How is Europe developing offshore wind energy?" (presentation at the Offshore Alternatives 2010 – MarineLog conference, March 2-3, 2010).

7. Walt Musial, National Wind Technology Center, "Offshore wind electricity: A viable energy option for the coastal United States," *Marine Technology Society Journal*, Fall 2007: 34.

8. *European Wind Energy Association, The European offshore wind industry – key trends and statistics 2009*, 5.

9. Rodgers, 44.

10. "Nysted Havmøllepark: The construction of Nysted offshore wind farm" brochure, 7-8, http://www. nystedwindfarm.com and http://www.dongenergy.com (accessed June 13, 2010).

11. Kevin Pearce, Stephen Geiger and Charles Nordstrom, "State of the Art in Offshore Wind Energy Projects" (paper published in the 2009 Annual Meeting Proceedings for the Society of Naval Architects and Marine Engineers), 2.

12. "Vestas Conducting Offshore, Energy-Storage Research Projects," *North American Windpower*, June 7, 2010.

13. Pearce, 2.

14. Brian Snyder and Mark J. Kaiser, "A comparison of offshore wind power development in Europe and the US: Patterns and drivers of development," *Applied Energy*, 2009: 1847.

15. Chris Gillis, "Offshore logistics specialist," *American Shipper*, May 2007: 21.

16. Kurt E. Thomsen, Gaoh Offshore Ltd., "Commentary: Developing the offshore energy future – Purpose-built vessels for the offshore wind industry," *Marine Technology Society Journal*, Summer 2008: 51.

17. *European Wind Energy Association, The European offshore wind industry – key trends and statistics 2009*, 12-13.

18. Musial, 34.

19. Gillis, 22.

20. Ibid, 20-21.

21. Ibid, 22.

22. Ibid, 24.

23. Drunsic, "How is Europe developing offshore wind energy?"

24. Community of Europe Shipyards' Associations, "Wind Power and Shipyard Industries Make Joint Call for Investments in Ships for Offshore Wind Expansion," February 25, 2010.

25. Torsten Thomas, "Smooth service in rough seas," *Sun & Wind Energy*, 2009: 114.

26. Ibid, 112.

27. Ibid, 114.

28. Chris Gillis, "No logistics breeze," *American Shipper*, April 2010: 15.

29. Jeremy van Loon, "Offshore Wind Boom as Utilities Seek 18% Margins," *Bloomberg/Businessweek*, April 30, 2010.

30. Gillis, "No logistics breeze," 15.

31. "Nysted Havmøllepark: The construction of Nysted offshore wind farm," 5.

32. Ian Gaitch, sales director, Global Marine Systems Energy. E-mail interview, February 10, 2010.

33. Ibid.

34. Ibid.

35. Ibid.

36. Simon-Philippe Breton and Geir Moe, "Status, plans and technologies for offshore wind turbines in Europe and North America," *Renewable Energy*, 2009: 646-647.

37. Stephen Rogers and Matthew Jackson. "Offshore wind: How to take action for a more uncertain future," *Power Engineering International*, December 2008: 31-33

38. E.ON UK, "Blyth is alive... producing power again," January 14, 2009.

39. Jan Behrendt Ibsoe, vice president, Renewable Energy Services, ABS Consulting, Houston, Texas. E-mail interview, February 3, 2010.

40. "Nysted Havmøllepark: The construction of Nysted offshore wind farm," 7.

41. Heinrich Duden, developer PTS (Personal Transfer System), and manager, ep4offshore, Winsen, Germany. E-mail interview, December 2, 2009.

42. Musial, 34.

43. Repower Systems AG, "REpower: First turbine for alpha ventus offshore wind farm installed," September 30, 2009.

44. Jörn Iken, "Going where it's rough," *Sun & Wind Energy*, 2008: 148.

45. Iken, 147.

46. Martin LaMonica, "Direct-drive turbines to propel offshore wind," *Green Tech*, April 30, 2010.

47. Richard Weiss, "GE to Debut Gearless Offshore Wind Turbine to Rival Siemens," *Bloomberg/Businessweek*, April 22, 2010.

Chapter 6

1. Mark Rodgers and Craig Olmsted, Cape Wind Associates, Boston, Massachusetts. "Engineering and regulatory challenges facing the development of commercially viable offshore wind projects," *Marine Technology Society Journal*, Summer 2008: 44.

2. Ibid, 46.

3. Ibid.

4. "Study: Cape Wind Will Reduce Regional Electricity Prices By $4.6 billion," *North American Windpower*, February 11, 2010.

5. Katie Zezima, "Interior Secretary Sees Little Hope for Consensus on Wind Farm," *The New York Times*, February 3, 2010.

6. Jay Lindsay. "Cape Wind's fate unclear, even in Obama's hands," *The Associated Press*, January 24, 2010.

7. "Secretary Salazar Announces Approval of Cape Wind Energy Project on Outer Continental Shelf of Massachusetts," U.S. Department of the Interior, April 28, 2010.

8. "Cape Wind Approved by Federal Government as America's First Offshore Wind Farm; Project will Add Clean Energy Jobs for Region," Cape Wind Associates, April 29, 2010.

9. "Lawsuits Take Aim at America's First Offshore Wind Farm," *Environmental News Service*, May 2, 2010.

10. "Cape Wind Signs Agreement to Buy Siemens 3.6-MW Offshore Wind Turbines," Cape Wind, March 31, 2010.

11. "National Grid and Cape Wind Sign Power Purchase Contract," National Grid, May 7, 2010.

12. Walt Musial, National Wind Technology Center, Golden, Colorado. "Offshore Wind Electricity: A Reliable Energy Option for the Coastal United States," *Marine Technology Society Journal,* Fall 2007: 33.

13. Ibid.

14. "Patrick Administration Releases Final Blueprint for Managing Development in State Waters," Executive Office of Energy and Environmental Affairs, Massachusetts, January 4, 2010.

15. Beth Daley. "State draws zones for coast wind farms," *The Boston Globe*, July 1, 2009.

16. "History of Hull's wind project," Hull Wind.org Web site, http://www.hullwind.org/history.php (accessed May 15, 2010).

17. Jay Fitzgerald. "Hull says offshore turbines too expensive," *Boston Herald*, May 11, 2010.

18. "Carcieri names Deepwater Wind as developer for Rhode Island's off-shore wind farm," Office of the Governor of Rhode Island, September 25, 2008.

19. Alex Kuffner. "Several companies want to be the first to develop an offshore wind farm in the U.S.," *The Providence Journal*, August 16, 2009.

20. Peter Voskamp, "PUC turns down wind farm contract," *The Block Island Times*, April 3, 2010.

21. Alex Kuffner. "Mixed views on Block Island over proposed wind farm," *The Providence Journal*, March 7, 2010.

22. "Garden State Offshore Energy wins bid for NJ offshore wind farm," Garden State Offshore Energy, October 3, 2008.

23. Jeffrey Ball. "Fish Juice: N.J. Fisherman angling to develop offshore wind," *The Wall Street Journal*, June 3, 2008.

24. Abby Gruen. "Preparation for groundbreaking offshore wind farm project begins in Atlantic City," *The Star-Ledger*, May 1, 2010.

25. Frank Eltman. "N.Y. utility scrapping ocean wind park," *The Associated Press*, August 24, 2007.

26. "LIPA and Con Edison form collaborative for major offshore wind initiative," Long Island Power Authority, April 20, 2009.

27. Ethan Wilensky-Lanford, "Baldacci pushes offshore wind," *Morning Sentinel*, May 12, 2010.

28. Ibid.

29. Steve Gelsi, "NRG Energy sees offshore wind revenue by 2014," *MarketWatch*, November 10, 2009.

30. "Interior Initiates Leasing Process for Commercial Wind Development on U.S. Outer Continental Shelf off Delaware," U.S. Department of the Interior, April 21, 2010.

31. Ibid.

32. Molly Murray, "University of Delaware, Feds to create research site for offshore wind energy," *DelawareOnline (The News Journal)*, June 12, 2010.

33. "University of Delaware, Gamesa Commission Wind Turbine," *North American Windpower*, June 14, 2010.

34. "Support Grows for Offshore Wind in Maryland," *Environment Maryland*, December 15, 2009.

35. Ibid.

36. Virginia Coastal Energy Research Consortium, Virginia Offshore Wind Studies, July 2007 to March 2010: Final Report, April 20, 2010, ix, http://www.vcerc.org/VCERC_Final_Report_Offshore_Wind_Studies_Full_Report_new.pdf (Accessed May 17, 2010).

37. Ibid, viii.

38. Steve Szkotak, "2 Va. firms seek to establish offshore wind farms," *The Associated Press*, February 25, 2010.

39. "Delaware, Maryland, Virginia sign wind power agreement," *Dover Post*, November 10, 2009.

40. John Murawski, "Outer Banks wind farm planned," *TheSunNews.com*, September 6, 2009.

41. Jim Brumm, "Duke Energy to fund offshore N. Carolina wind project," *Reuters*, October 6, 2009.

42. "Santee Cooper Green – Wind Power," Santee Cooper Web site, http://www.santeecoopergreen.com (accessed May 18, 2010).

43. Bob Keefe, "Feds eye wind power off Georgia coast," *The Atlanta Journal-Constitution*, April 2, 2009.

44. "U.S. Wind Energy Projects" (as of December 31, 2009), American Wind Energy Association Web site, http://www.awea.org/projects (accessed May 30, 2010).

45. Richard Slawsky, "Abandoned rigs could house wind farm," *New Orleans City Business*, September 27, 2004.

46. Ibid.

47. *U.S. Offshore Wind Energy: A Path Forward* (a working paper for the U.S. Offshore Wind Collaborative), October 2009, 14.

48. Christopher Gillis, *Windpower* (Atglen, Pennsylvania: Schiffer Publishing Ltd., 2008), 79-80.

49. "Texas Grants Largest Offshore Wind Concessions in the USA," Baryonyx Corporation, July 16, 2009.

50. "NaiKun Wind project receives environmental approval," NaiKun Wind Energy Group, December 10, 2009.

51. "NaiKun Wind takes steps to sustain offshore wind project, announces second quarter financial results," NaiKun Wind Energy Group, May 20, 2010.

52. Catherine A. Cardno, "Institute releases study of Michigan's offshore wind potential," *Civil Engineering,* December 2008: 14-15.

53. Kevin Braciszeski, "Lake Michigan wind farm a tough sell," *Ludington Daily News*, December 16, 2009.

54. Dave Alexander, "Offshore wind farm developer scaling back plans," *Muskegon Chronicle*, February 13, 2010.

55. Kari Lydersen, "Studies lift hopes for Great Lakes wind turbine farms," *The Washington Post*, October 7, 2008.

56. Robert H. Owen Jr., president, Superior Safety and Environmental Services Inc., Middleton, Wisconsin, Final Report to Wisconsin Focus on Energy on Energy on Lake Michigan Offshore Wind Resource Assessment (funded by the Wisconsin Focus on Energy Program) (July 30, 2004), 61.

57. *U.S. Offshore Wind Energy: A Path Forward*, 16.

58. "Great Lakes Wind Energy Center Final Feasibility Report," Cuyahoga County Department of Development, Ohio, Web site, http://www.development.cuyahogacounty.us/en-US/name.aspx (accessed May 22, 2010).

59. John Funk, "5 turbines in the works for wind power project in Lake Erie," *The Plain Dealer*, May 24, 2010.

60. "GE and Lake Erie Energy Development Corporation Announce Great Lakes Offshore Wind Partnership at AWEA," GE Power & Water, May 24, 2010.

61. ""NYPA President Kessel calls for Proposals to Develop the First Fresh Water Wind Energy Initiative in the Nation: Increasing Emissions-Free Wind Power will Contribute to Cleaner Air and Job Growth," New York Power Authority, December 1, 2009.

62. Lisa Wood, "Trillium plans massive Great Lakes wind farms at initial cost estimate of $8 billion," *Electric Utility Week*, August 3, 2009.

63. Jeff Long, "Evanston takes a look at wind turbines in Lake Michigan," *Chicago Tribune*, April 14, 2010.

64. Wood, *Electric Utility Week*.

65. Chris Gillis, "No logistics breeze," *American Shipper,* April 2010: 14-15.

66. Ibid, 16-18.

67. "Port Corpus Christi to sell Ingleside facility," *American Shipper*, May 21, 2010.

68. Brian Snyder and Mark J. Kaiser, "A comparison of offshore wind power development in Europe and the US: Patterns and drivers of development," *Applied Energy,* 2009: 1853.

69. Jim Efstanthiou Jr. "Offshore Wind Farms in U.S. Should Be Linked, Researchers Say," *Bloomberg*, April 5, 2010.

70. Memorandum of Understanding Between the United States Department of the Interior and the States of Maine, New Hampshire, Massachusetts, Rhode Island, New York, New Jersey, Delaware, Maryland, Virginia, North Carolina to Create an Atlantic Offshore Wind Energy Consortium To Coordinate Issues of Regional Applicability for the Purpose of Promoting the Efficient, Expeditious, Orderly and Responsible Development of the Wind Resources of the Atlantic Outer Continental Shelf, U.S. Department of the Interior, June 8, 2010.

Chapter 7

1. Hikaru Matsumiya, professor, Japanese wind energy industry, Tokyo, Japan. E-mail interview, February 4, 2010.

2. Ibid.

3. Peter Fairley. "Chinese Wind Power Heads Offshore," *M.I.T. Review*, April 5, 2010.

4. Ron Mahabir. "Japan follows Europe by tapping offshore wind for power," *Asia Clean Energy & Asia Clean Technology News*, January 21, 2008.

5. U.K. Department of Energy & Climate Change, London, United Kingdom, "New player in UK offshore wind market," February 25, 2010.

6. Wan Zhihong. "Nation eyes offshore wind power," *China Daily*, December 10, 2007.

7. He Dexin, president, Chinese Wind Energy Association, "Brief introduction of wind energy development in China," Beijing, China, e-mail interview with author, December 17, 2009.

8. Ibid.

9. Ibid.

10. "China speeds up offshore wind power construction," *Xinhua News Agency*, March 19, 2010.

11. Fairley, "Chinese Wind Power Heads Offshore."

12. Global Wind Energy Council, Brussels, Belgium, "The New Rules of Chinese Offshore Project Development," interview, February 23, 2010.

13. Fairley, "Chinese Wind Power Heads Offshore."

14. Global Wind Energy Council, interview.

15. Fairley, "Chinese Wind Power Heads Offshore."

16. G. Li, "Feasibility of large scale offshore wind power for Hong Kong – a preliminary study," *Renewable Energy* (November/December 2000): 388.

17. Ibid.

18. John Duce, "CLP gets approval to develop Hong Kong wind farm," *Bloomberg.com*, August 3, 2009.

19. Cheng-Dar Yue and Min-How Yang, "Exploring the potential of wind energy for a coastal state," *Energy Policy*, 2009: 3930.

20. "Offshore Wind Project Planned for Taiwan," *Renewable Energy World*, October 27, 2009.

21. "Wind farm planned for Taiwan Strait," *The Engineer*, February 10, 2010.

22. Hyun-Goo Kim, Wind Energy Research Center, Korea Institute of Energy Research, Seoul, South Korea, "Onshore/offshore wind resource potential of South Korea," http://www.ewec2009proceedings.info/allfiles2/30_EWEC2009presentation.pdf (accessed February 10, 2010.

23. Rhee So-eui. "Playing catch-up, now wind power firms head offshore," *Reuters*, December 4, 2009.

24. Kim Tae-gyu, "Korea eyes massive wind farm on western coast," *Korea Times*, February 7, 2010.

25. M. V, Ramsurya. "India's wind power draws global majors," *The Economic Times*, April 26, 2010.

26. Sindya N. Bhanoo. "Report predicts offshore wind boom," *The New York Times – Green Inc.*, December 31, 2009.

27. "New Report: Offshore Wind Power Could Increase To 55 GW By 2020," *North American Windpower*, August 24, 2009.

Chapter 8

1. "Aerodynamic Wind Mills," *Scientific American*, June 1929: 525.

2. Christopher Gillis. *Windpower* (Atglen, Pennsylvania: Schiffer Publishing Ltd., 2008), 27.

3. Craig Toepfer. *The Hybrid Electric Home* (Atglen, Pennsylvania: Schiffer Publishing Ltd., 2010), 69.

4. Ibid, 64.

5. Gillis, 28.

6. Toepfer, 66-67.

7. Gillis, 31.

8. Ibid.

9. Ibid, 33.

10. Ibid, 34.

11. Ibid.

12. Scott Dine. "Sailing off the Grid: Wind, Water and Sun Sustain Sailors," *Bay Weekly Online*, October 4-10, 2001.

13. Ampair, Warfield, United Kingdom, Web site http://www.ampair.com, "Our history" (accessed April 23, 2010).

14. Dine, 2001.

15. Pete Anderson, president, Eclectic Energy Ltd., Ollerton, United Kingdom, e-mail interview with author, June 2, 2010.

16. Dine, 2001.

17. "Offshore Log: A Caribbean-built Wind Generator," *Practical Sailor*, September 1, 1998.

18. Ampair Web site http://www.ampair.com.

19. Anderson, interview.

20. Ibid.

21. Ibid.

22. Ibid.

23. Chris Gillis and Philip Damas, "Vessel operators ride green wave," *American Shipper*, August 2004: 86.

24. Gillis, Windpower, 38-39.

25. Southwest Windpower, Flagstaff, Arizona. Website: www.windenergy.com (accessed May 1, 2010).

26. Andy Kruse, senior vice president, business development, Southwest Windpower, Flagstaff, Arizona. E-mail interview, May 1, 2010.

Chapter 9
1. Adam Aston. "The war over offshore wind is almost over," *Business Week*, July 7, 2008: 52-55.

2. Ibid.

3. Beth Daley. "2 tribes object to Cape Wind turbines," *The Boston Globe*, October 26, 2009.

4. Robert Thompson. "Reporting offshore wind power: Are newspapers facilitating informal debate?" *Coastal Management*, 2005: 254.

5. Jeremy Firestone and Willett Kempton. "Public opinion about large offshore wind power: Underlying factors," *Energy Policy*, March 2007: 1596.

6. Chris Gillis. "Left out," *American Shipper*, April 2010: 16.

7. Brian Braginton-Smith, The Conservation Consortium, South Yarmouth, Massachusetts. "Commentary: Offshore Wind Energy, Frontier Outposts for Sustainable Seas," *Marine Technology Society Journal*, Winter 2002: 12.

8. "Santee Cooper releases offshore wind turbine simulation photos," SCnow.com, http://www2.scnow.com (accessed November 5, 2009).

9. Walt Musial, National Wind Technology Center, Golden, Colorado. "Offshore Wind Electricity: A Viable Energy Option for the Coastal United States," *Marine Technology Society Journal*, Fall 2007: 34.

10. Jacob Ladenburg. "Willingness to pay for reduced visual disamenities from offshore wind farms in Denmark," *Energy Policy*, 2007: 4059.

11. Gillis, 16.

12. Mark Rodgers and Craig Olmsted, Cape Wind Associates, Boston, Massachusetts. "Engineering and regulatory challenges facing the development of commercially viable offshore wind projects," *Marine Technology Society Journal*, Summer 2008: 49.

13. Christine Boesen, Energi E2, Copenhagen, Denmark, "Environmental monitoring at Nysted and Horns Rev offshore wind farms," (presentation made at the Great Lakes Offshore Gathering, Toledo, Ohio, April 4, 2006).

14. Tabor D. Allison, Ellen Jedrey, and Simon Perkins, Massachusetts Audubon Society, Lincoln, Massachusetts. "Avian issues for offshore wind development," *Marine Technology Society Journal*, Summer 2008: 34.

15. Tux Turkel. "Will birds and wind farms compete?" *Portland Press Herald*, May 31, 2010.

16. Allison, 33.

17. Morten Milthers, senior consultant, Wind and Water Maritime Consultants, Svendborg, Denmark. E-mail interview, January 5, 2010.

18. Strandingmuseum St. George, Ulfborg, Denmark. Website: www.strandmus.dk/uk-version/index-uk.htm (accessed June 14, 2010).

19. Milthers, interview.

20. Allister Doyle. "Stone Age could complicate N. Sea wind farm plans," *Reuters*, March 23, 2010.

21. Milthers, interview.

Chapter 10

1. Roger Hamilton. "Can We Harness The Wind?" *National Geographic,* December 1975: 825.

2. Paul Sclavounos, professor, Department of Mechanical Engineering, Massachusetts Institute of Technology, Cambridge, Massachusetts. "Floating offshore wind turbines," *Marine Technology Society Journal,* Summer 2008: 39.

3. Theodore Lilas and Nikitakos, Department of Shipping Trade and Transport, University of the Aegean, and Antanasios Vatistas, Ecowindwater Ltd., Greece. "Floating Wind Turbine: Floating, Autonomous, Environmentally Friendly and Efficient Desalination Unit," *Windtech International,* April/May 2008: 9.

4. Theodore Lilas, Department of Shipping Trade and Transport, University of the Aegean, Chios, Greece. E-mail interview, January 15, 2010.

5. Dominque Roddier and Joshua Weinstein. "Floating wind turbines," *Mechanical Engineering,* April 2010: 4-5.

6. Ibid, 4.

7. Peter Fairley. "Wind Power That Floats," *Technology Review* (Massachusetts Institute of Technology, Cambridge, Massachusetts), April 2, 2008.

8. "Floating Wind Turbines," *Offshore Industry,* 2009: 51.

9. Fairley, "Wind Power That Floats."

10. Jörn Iken. "Deepwater – only for swimmers!" *Sun & Wind Energy,* 2008: 151.

11. Statoil, Stavanger, Norway. "Statoil Hydro inaugurates floating wind turbine," September 8, 2009.

12. Dominque Roddier, naval architect and founder of offshore engineering firm Marine Innovation & Technology, and chief technology officer, Principle Power Inc., Seattle, Washington. Telephone interview, March 11, 2010.

13. Roddier and Weinstein, "Floating wind turbines," 6.

14. Ibid.

15. Roddier, interview.

16. SWAY, Rådal, Norway, Web site http://www.sway.no (accessed March 19, 2010).

17. Enova, Trondheim, Norway, "Enova pledges NOK 137 million to innovative offshore wind turbine from SWAY," February 12, 2010.

18. Larry Viterna, president and chief executive officer, Nautica Windpower, Olmsted Falls, Ohio. E-mail interview, February 15, 2010.

19. Fairley, "Wind Power That Floats."

20. Energy Technologies Institute, Loughborough, United Kingdom, "ETI NOVA Project Statement," January 13, 2009.

21. William E. Heronemus and Woody Stoddard, Ocean Wind Energy Systems, Inc., Amherst, Massachusetts, "Simple Arrays of Wind Turbines as a Practical Alternative to the Single Large Rotor Machines" (Presentation at Windpower 2003, Austin Texas).

22. Ibid.

23. OWES, LLC, Tulsa, Oklahoma, Business Plan, October 2009, 64.

24. Ibid, 65.

25. Marcia A. Heronemus-Pate, managing member, OWES, LLC, Tulsa, Oklahoma. Telephone interview, December 10, 2009.

26. Heronemus-Pate, e-mail interview, May 5, 2010.

27. Ibid.

Index